EASY GUITAR
WITH NOTES & TAB

ROCK BAND

ISBN 978-1-4234-3934-9

HAL•LEONARD®
CORPORATION
7777 W. BLUEMOUND RD. P.O. BOX 13819 MILWAUKEE, WI 53213

Visit Hal Leonard Online at
www.halleonard.com

Are You Gonna Be My Girl

Words and Music by Nic Cester and Cameron Muncey

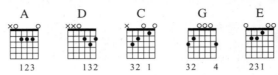

Strum Pattern: 2
Pick Pattern: 3

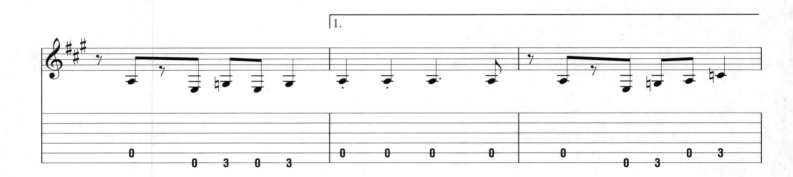

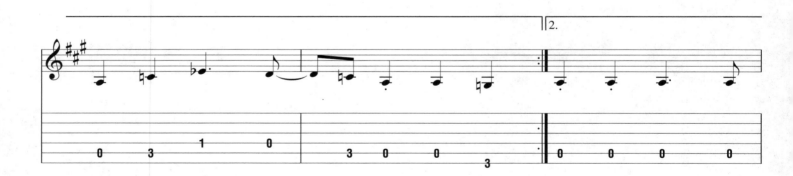

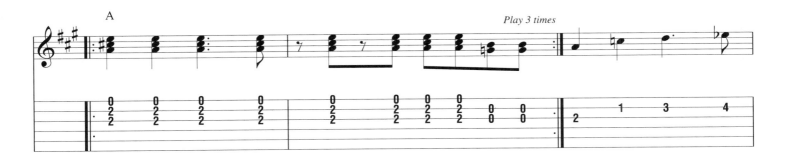

Verse

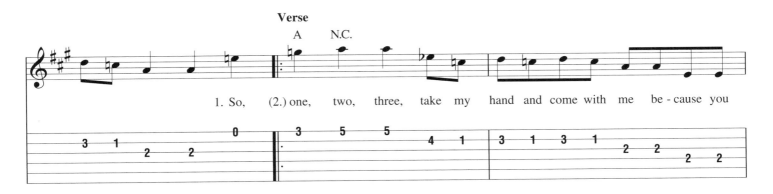

1. So, (2.) one, two, three, take my hand and come with me be-cause you

look so fine that I real - ly wan - na make you mine.

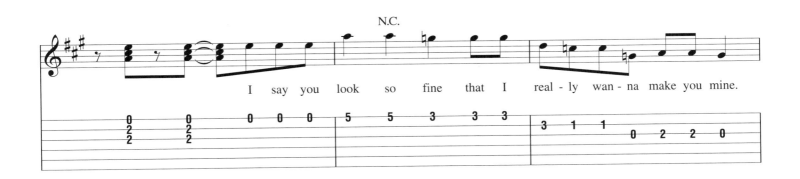

I say you look so fine that I real - ly wan - na make you mine.

Well, four, five, six, come on ___

_____ and get your kicks. Now you don't need the mon - ey { when you / with a

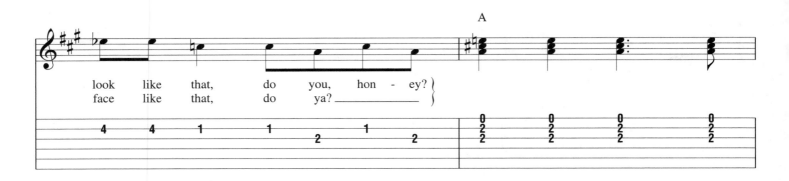

A

look like that, do you, hon - ey? }
face like that, do ya? _____ }

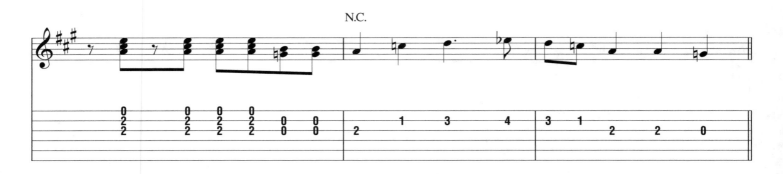

N.C.

Pre-Chorus

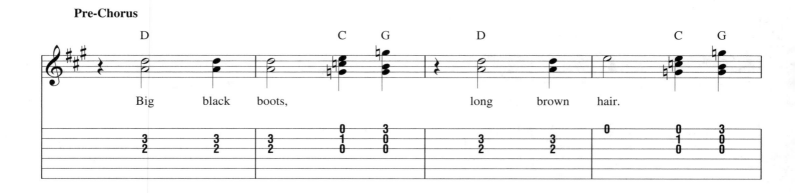

D   C   G   D   C   G

Big   black   boots,   long   brown   hair.

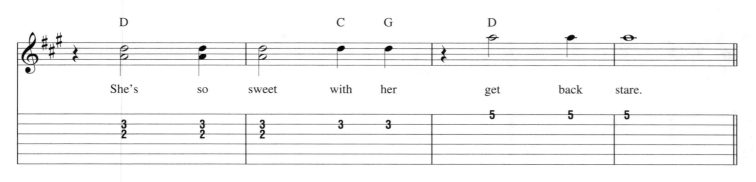

D   C   G   D

She's   so   sweet   with   her   get   back   stare.

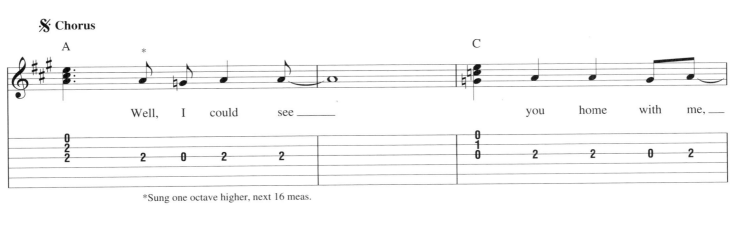

*Sung one octave higher, next 16 meas.

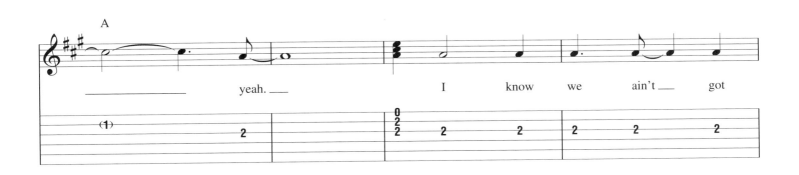

To Coda ⊕

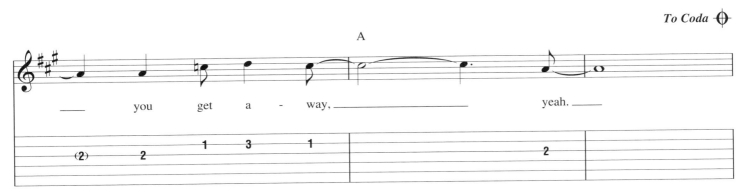

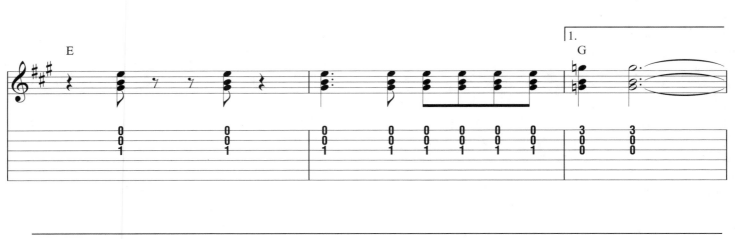

I said, "Are you gon-na be _____ my girl?"

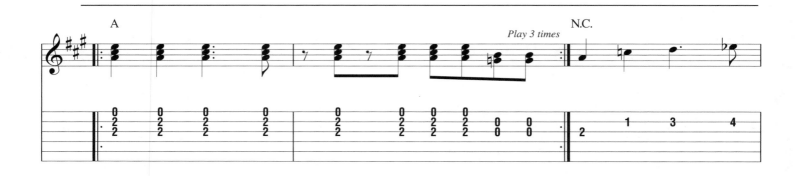

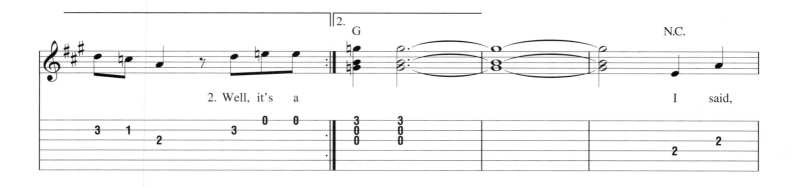

2. Well, it's a I said,

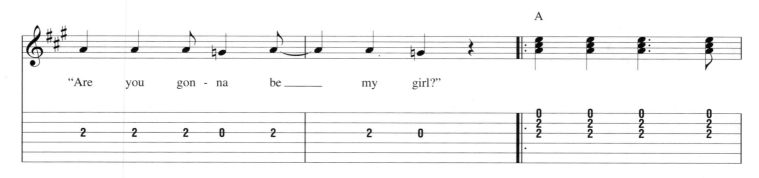

"Are you gon-na be _____ my girl?"

Guitar Solo

Play 4 times

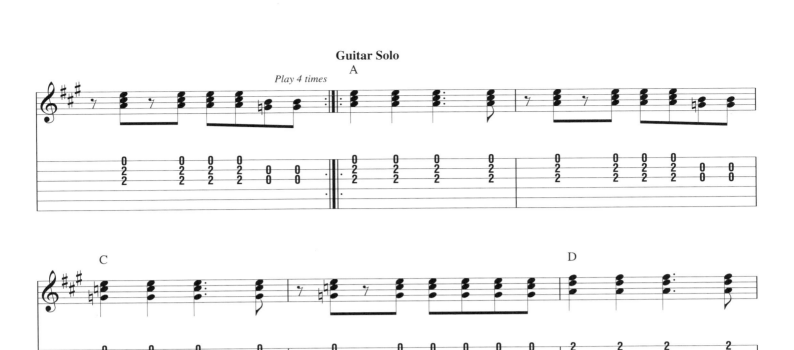

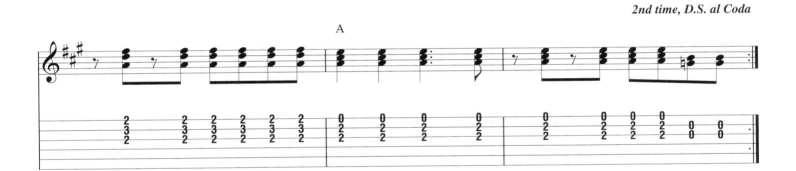

2nd time, D.S. al Coda

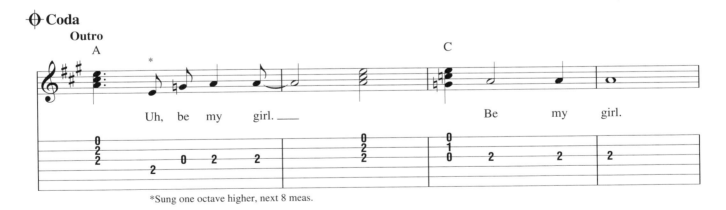

Coda

Outro

Uh, be my girl. _____ Be my girl.

*Sung one octave higher, next 8 meas.

Are you gon - na be _____ my girl? _____

Black Hole Sun

Words and Music by Chris Cornell

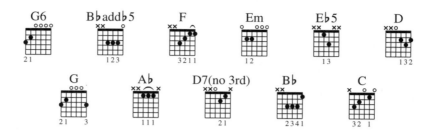

Strum Pattern: 3
Pick Pattern: 3

Verse

Slow Rock

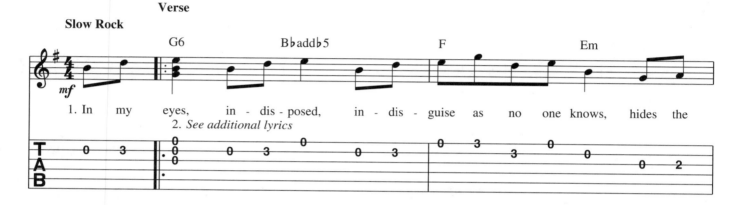

1. In my eyes, in - dis - posed, in - dis - guise as no one knows, hides the
2. *See additional lyrics*

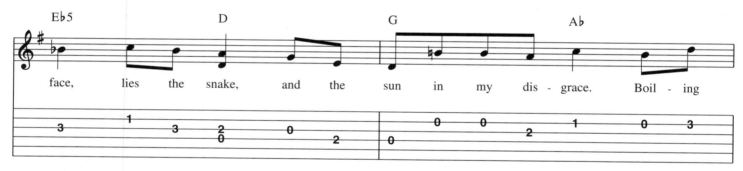

face, lies the snake, and the sun in my dis - grace. Boil - ing

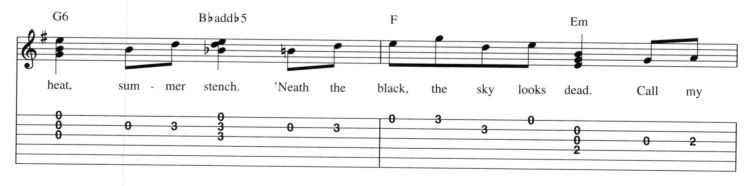

heat, sum - mer stench. 'Neath the black, the sky looks dead. Call my

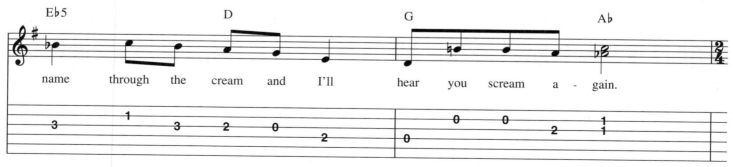

name through the cream and I'll hear you scream a - gain.

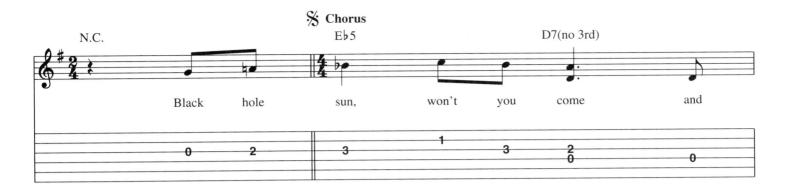

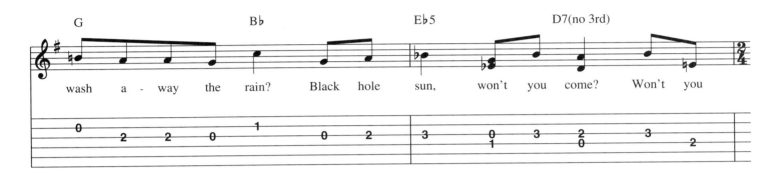

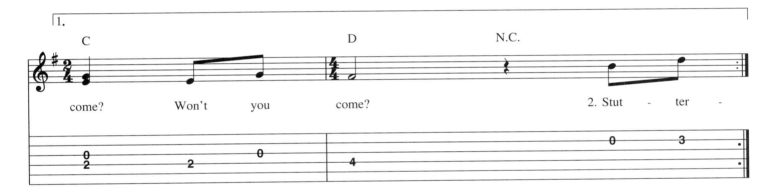

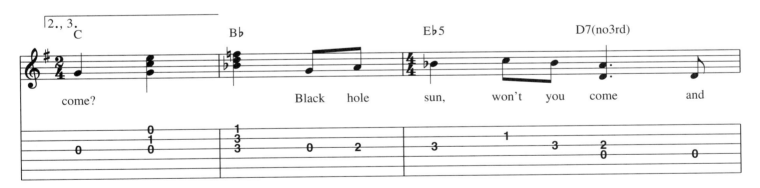

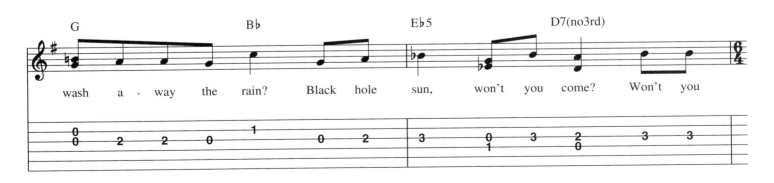

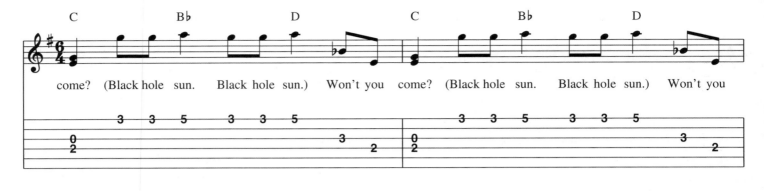

come? (Black hole sun. Black hole sun.) Won't you come? (Black hole sun. Black hole sun.) Won't you

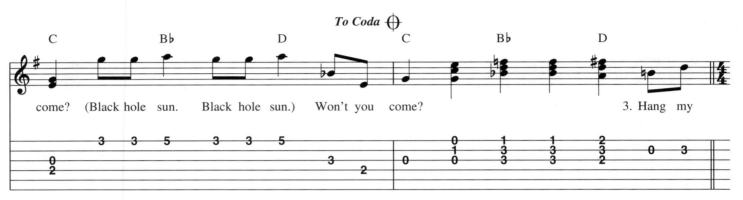

To Coda ⊕

come? (Black hole sun. Black hole sun.) Won't you come? 3. Hang my

Verse

D.S. al Coda

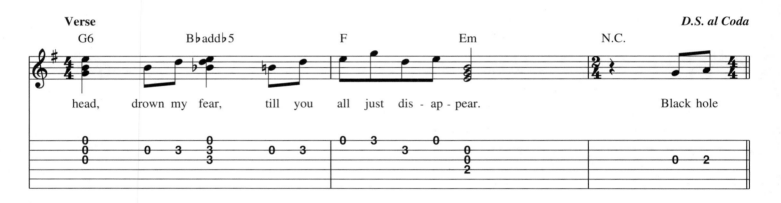

head, drown my fear, till you all just dis-ap-pear. Black hole

⊕ **Coda**

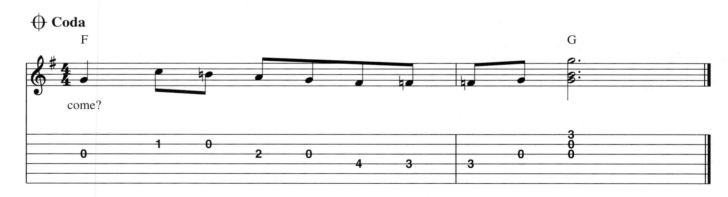

come?

Additional Lyrics

2. Stuttering, cold and damp.
   Steal the warm wind, tired friend.
   Times are gone for honest men,
   And sometimes far too long for snakes.
   In my shoes, a walking sleep.
   In my youth I pray to keep.
   Heaven send hell away.
   No one sings like you anymore.

Creep

Words and Music by Albert Hammond, Mike Hazlewood, Thomas Yorke, Richard Greenwood, Philip Selway, Colin Greenwood and Edward O'Brian

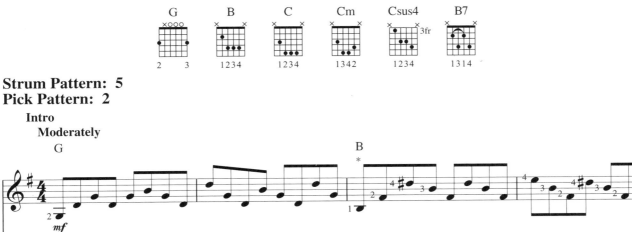

Strum Pattern: 5
Pick Pattern: 2

Intro
Moderately

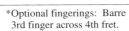

*Optional fingerings: Barre
3rd finger across 4th fret.

1. When you were here __ be-fore, __

**As before: 5th fret

Verse

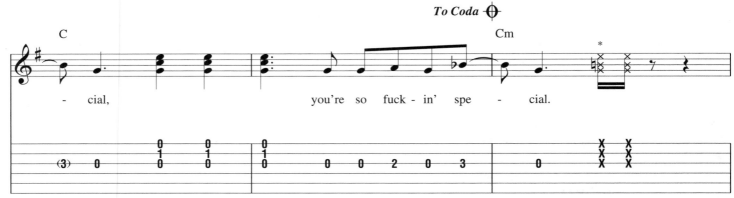

*Muffled strings: Lay the fret
hand across the strings with-
out depressing and strike them
w/ the pick hand.

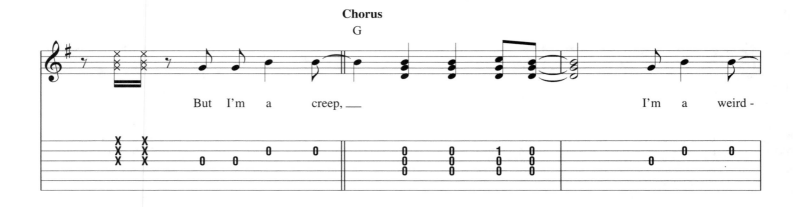

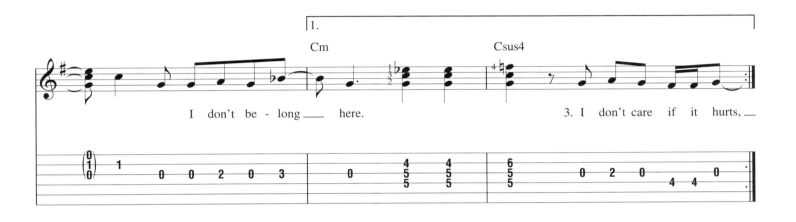

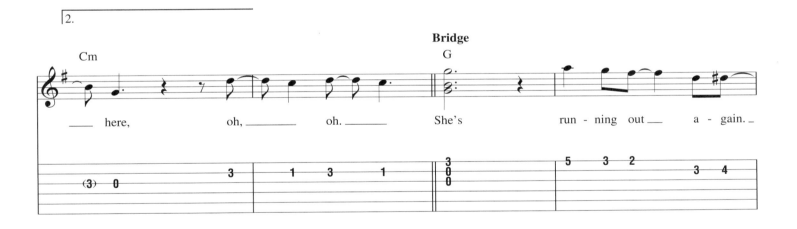

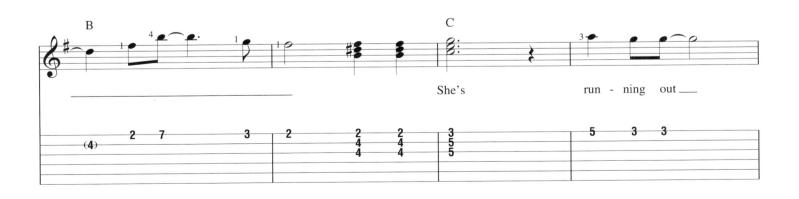

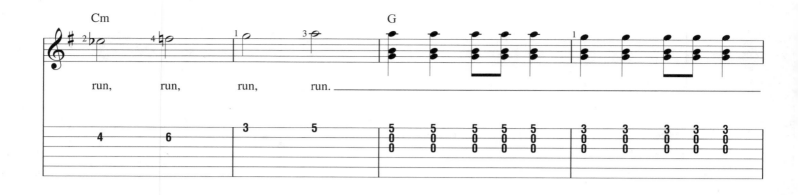

run,   run,   run,   run.

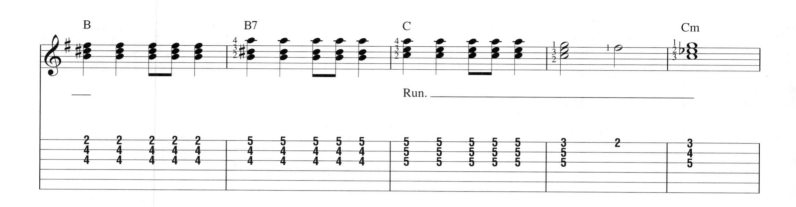

Run.

D.S. al Coda   Coda

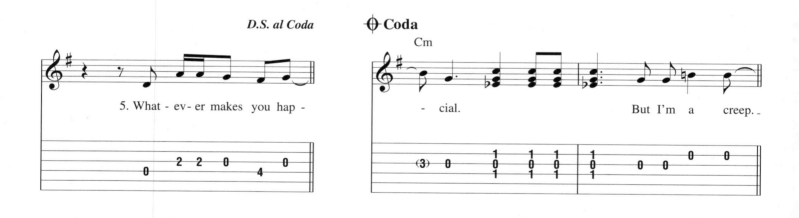

5. What - ev- er makes you hap -   - cial.   But I'm a   creep..

Outro-Chorus

I'm a   weird - o.

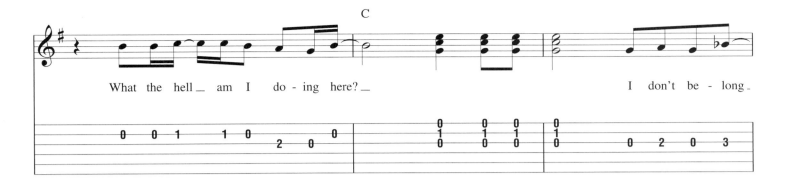

What the hell __ am I do - ing here? __   I don't be - long __

__ here.   I don't be - long _____ here.

Additional Lyrics

3. I don't care if it hurts,
   I want to have control.
   I want a perfect body,
   I want a perfect soul.

4. I want you to notice
   When I'm not around.
   You're so fuckin' special,
   I wish I were special.

5. Whatever makes you happy,
   Whatever you want.
   You're so fuckin' special,
   I wish I were special.

Dani California

Words and Music by Anthony Kiedis, Flea, John Frusciante and Chad Smith

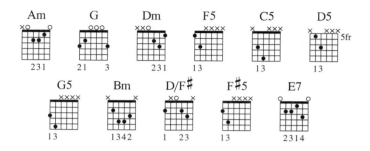

Strum Pattern: 3, 5

Intro
Moderately

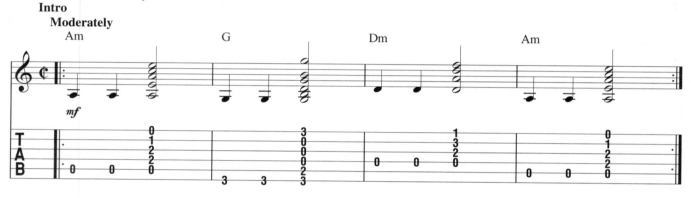

Verse

cont. rhy. sim.

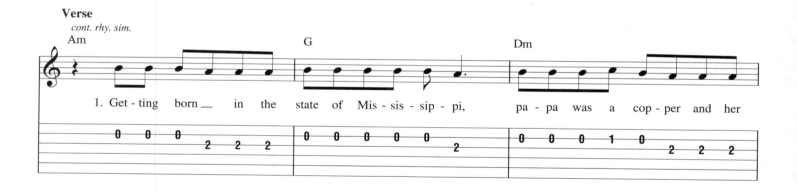

1. Get-ting born — in the state of Mis-sis-sip-pi, pa-pa was a cop-per and her

mam-ma was a hip-pie. In Al-a-bam-a, she ___ would swing a ham-mer.

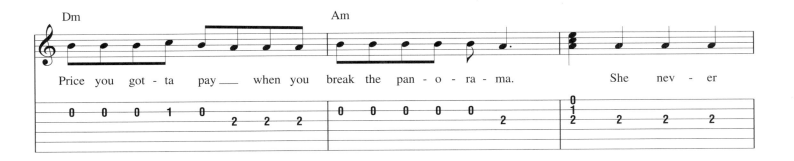

Price you got - ta pay __ when you break the pan - o - ra - ma. She nev - er

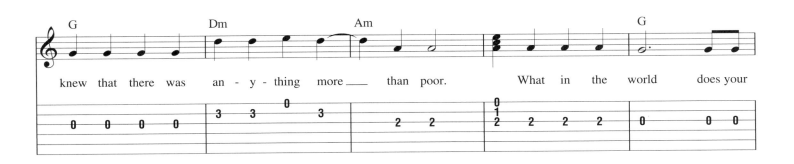

knew that there was an - y - thing more __ than poor. What in the world does your

𝄋 **Verse**

com - pa - ny take __ me for? 2. Black ban - dan - na, sweet __ Lou - i - si - an - a,
3. *See additional lyrics*

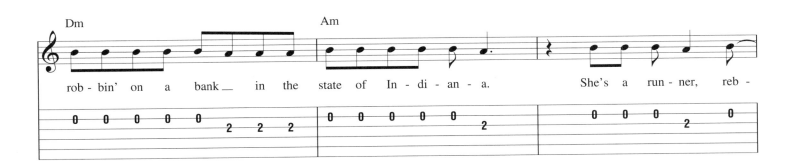

rob - bin' on a bank __ in the state of In - di - an - a. She's a run - ner, reb -

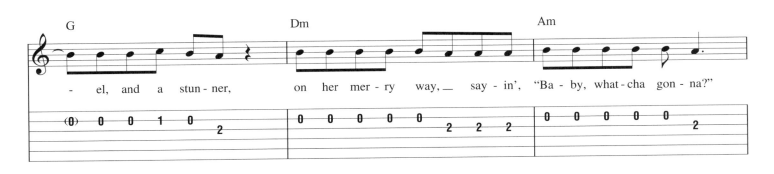

- el, and a stun - ner, on her mer - ry way, __ say - in', "Ba - by, what - cha gon - na?"

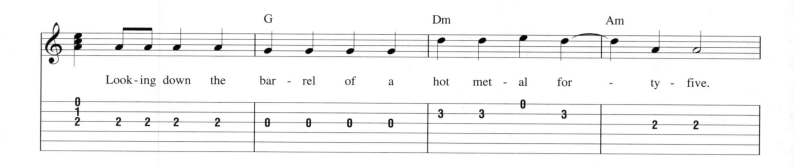

Look-ing down the bar-rel of a hot met - al for - ty - five.

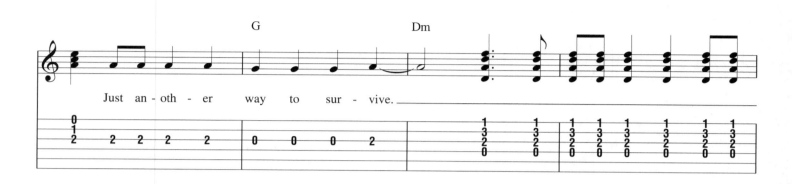

Just an - oth - er way to sur - vive.

𝄋𝄋 Chorus

Cal - i - for - nia, rest ___ in peace. ___ Si - mul - ta -

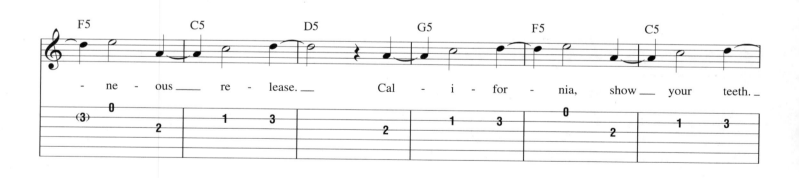

- ne - ous ___ re - lease. ___ Cal - i - for - nia, show ___ your teeth. ___

To Coda 2 ⊕

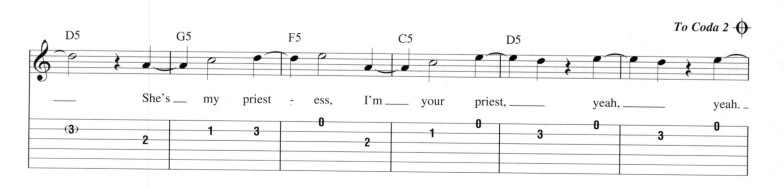

___ She's ___ my priest - ess, I'm ___ your priest, ___ yeah, ___ yeah. ___

20

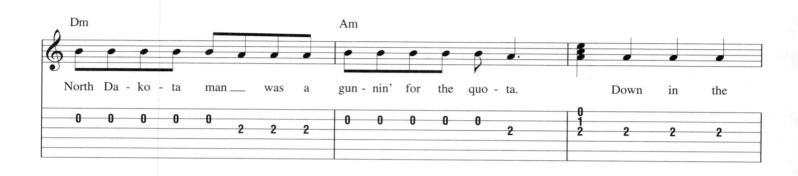

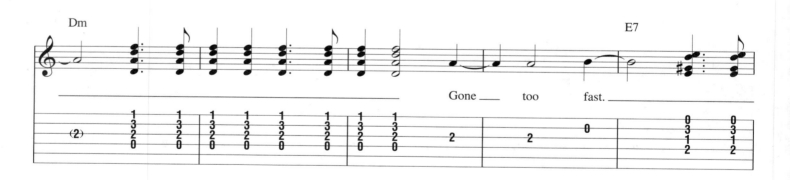

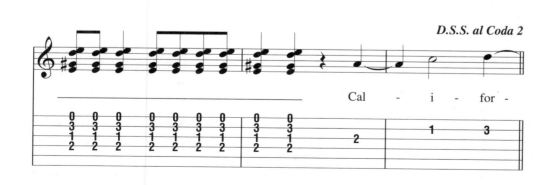

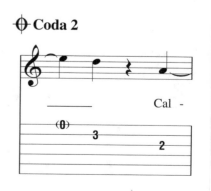

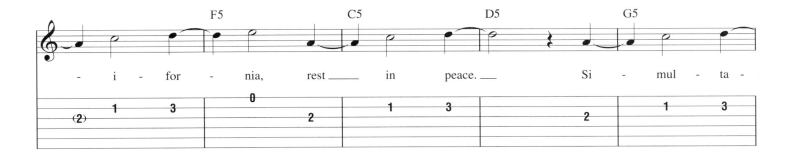

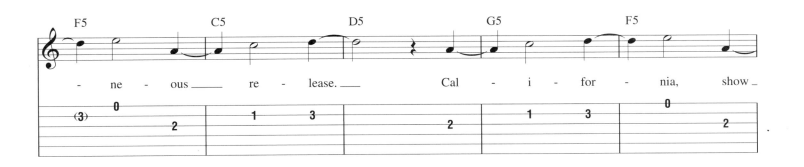

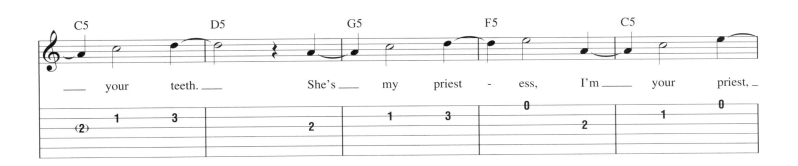

Additional Lyrics

3. She's a lover, baby, and a fighter.
   Should-a seen her comin' when it got a little brighter.
   With a name like Dani California, (the)
   Day was gonna come when I was gonna mourne ya.
   A little loaded, she was stealin' another breath.
   I love my baby to death.

Detroit Rock City

Words and Music by Paul Stanley and Bob Ezrin

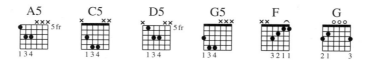

Strum Pattern: 1
Pick Pattern: 1

Intro

Fast Rock

1. I feel up - tight on a
2. Get - tin' late, I
3., 4. *See additional lyrics*

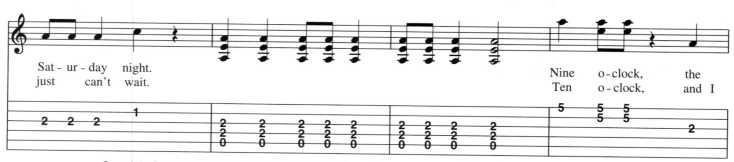

Sat - ur - day night.
just can't wait.

Nine o-clock, the
Ten o-clock, and I

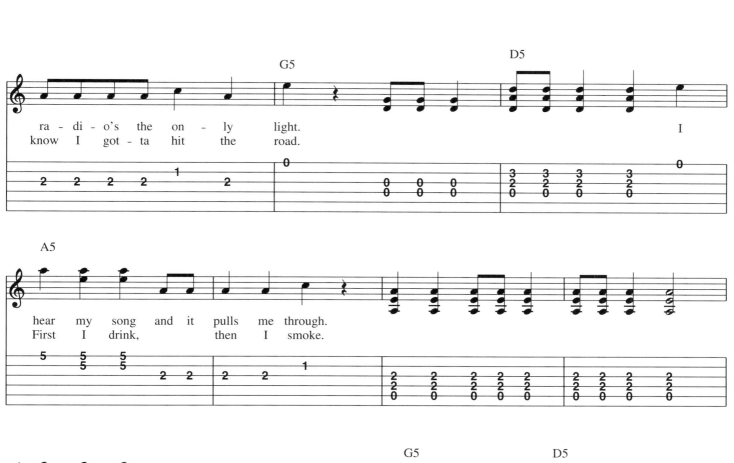

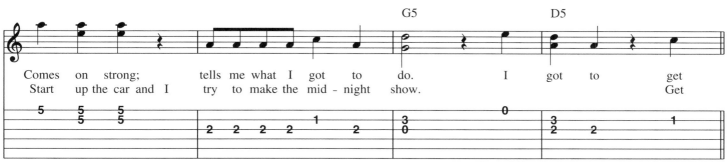

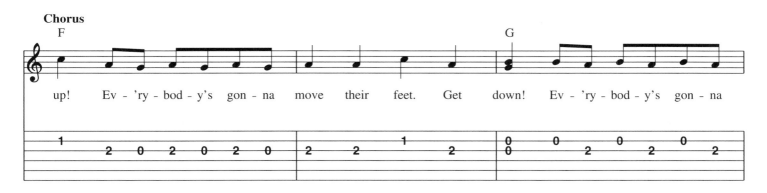

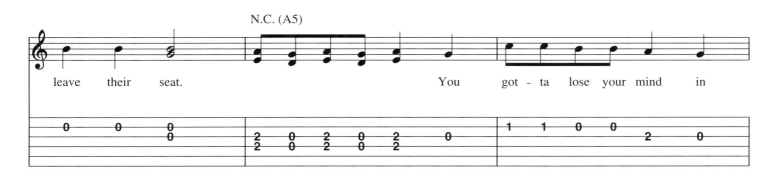

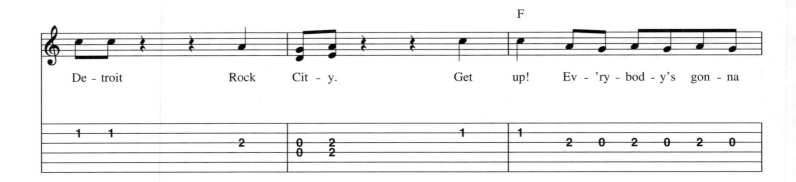

De - troit   Rock   Cit - y.   Get   up!   Ev - 'ry - bod - y's   gon - na

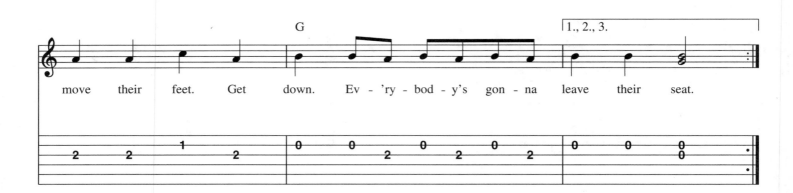

move   their   feet.   Get   down.   Ev - 'ry - bod - y's   gon - na   leave   their   seat.

Get   up!   Ev - 'ry - bod - y's   gon - na

leave   their   seat.   Get   down!

Additional Lyrics

3. Movin' fast doin' ninety five.
   Hit top speed, but I'm still movin' much too slow.
   Feel so good; I'm so alive.
   Hear my song, playin' on the radio. It goes;

4. Twelve o'clock, I gotta rock.
   There's a truck ahead, lights starin' at my eyes.
   Whoa, my God, no time to turn,
   I got to laugh, 'cause I know I'm gonna die. Why?

Don't Fear the Reaper

Words and Music by Donald Roeser

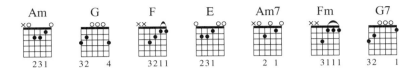

Strum Pattern: 3
Pick Pattern: 2

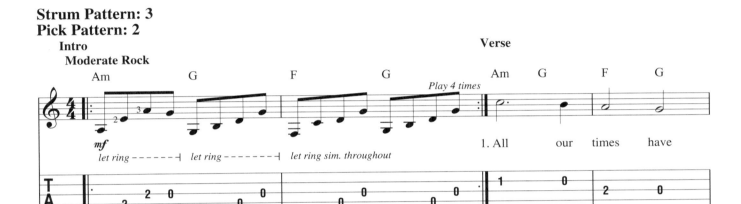

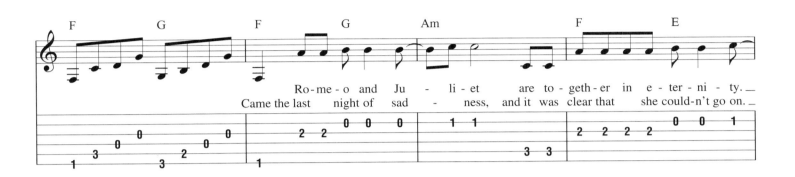

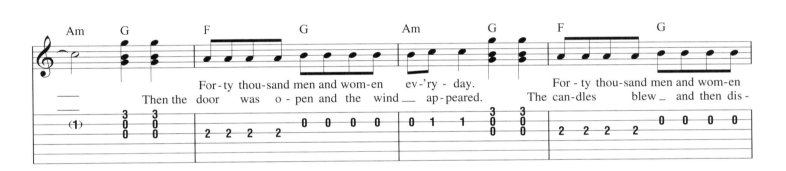

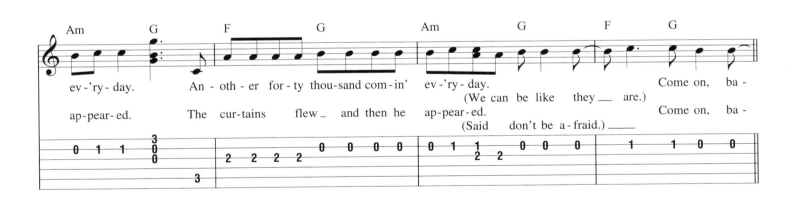

Chorus
F E Am G F G Am G
wind, the sun or the rain. (We can be like they are.) Come on, ba - by. (Don't fear the reap -
F G Am G F G Am G
- er.) Ba - by, take my hand. (Don't fear the reap - er.) We'll be a - ble to fly. (Don't fear the reap -
F G Am G F G Am G F G Am G
- er.) Ba - by, I'm your man. La, la, la, la, la.
F G Am G F G *Am7
*Let chord ring.
Interlude
Am G F G
Play 4 times
Verse
Am G F G
2. Val - en - tine is
3. Love of two is

Chorus

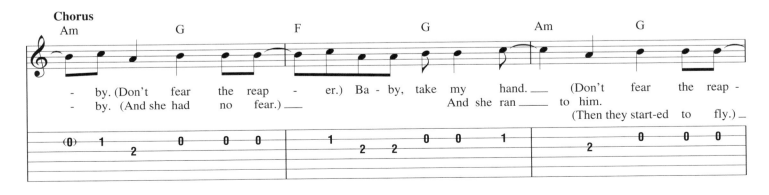

-er.) We'll be a - ble to fly.____ (Don't fear the reap - er.) Ba - by, I'm your man.____
They looked back-ward and said ____ good-bye. She had ta - ken his hand.____
(She had be-come like they ____ are.)

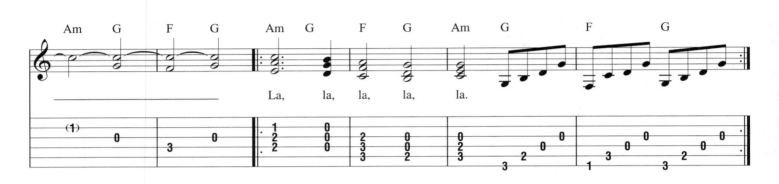

La, la, la, la, la.

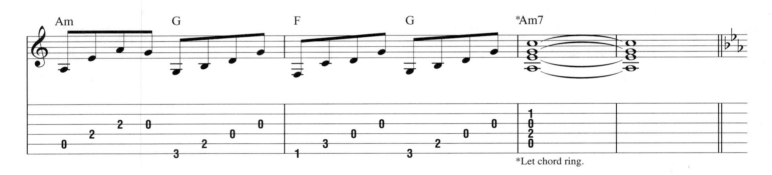

*Let chord ring.

Bridge

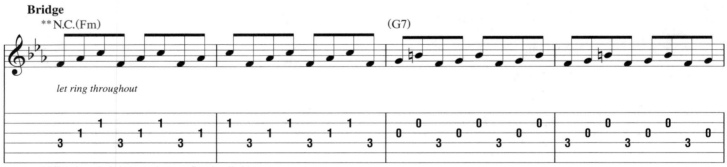

let ring throughout

**Chord symbols in parentheses reflect implied harmony.

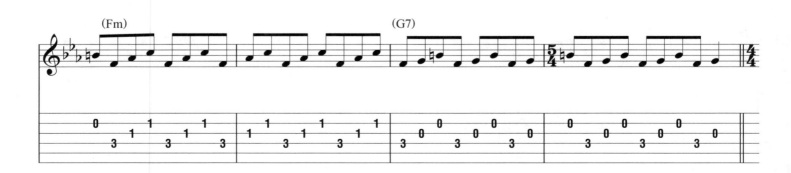

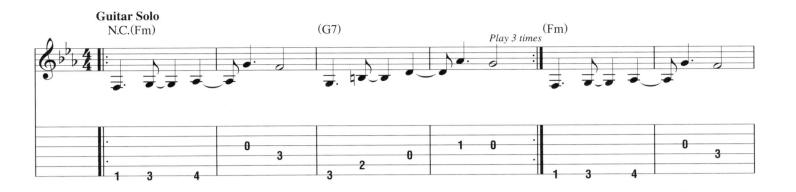

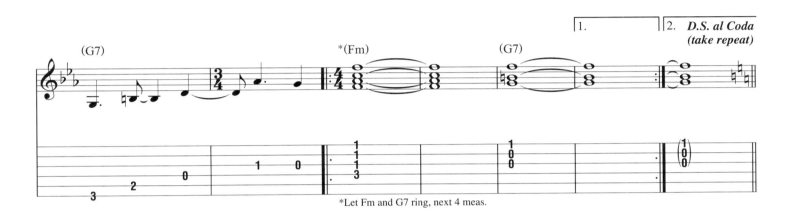

*Let Fm and G7 ring, next 4 meas.

Green Grass and High Tides

Words and Music by Hugh Thomasson Jr.

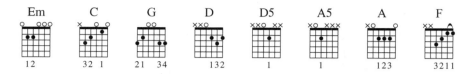

Strum Pattern: 3, 4
Pick Pattern: 3, 4

Intro
Moderate Rock

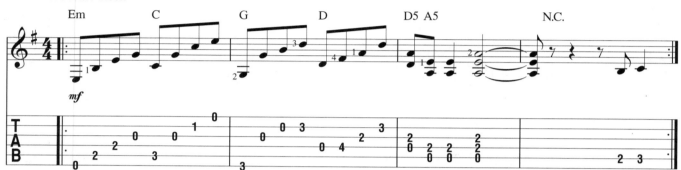

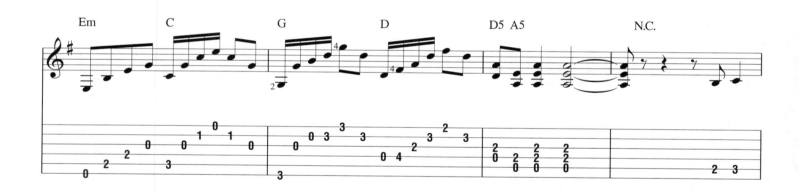

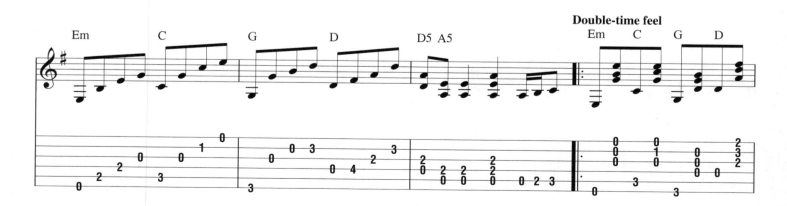

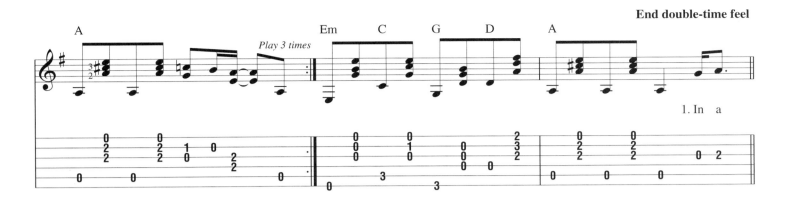

Verse

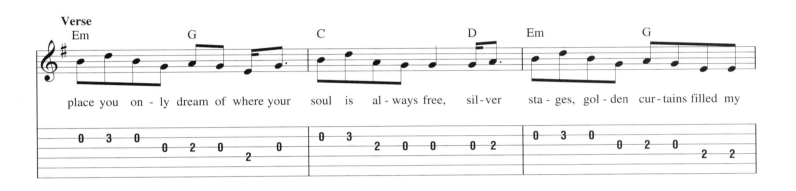

place you on - ly dream of where your soul is al - ways free, sil - ver sta - ges, gol - den cur - tains filled my

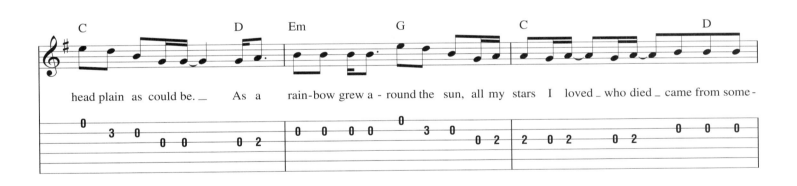

head plain as could be. __ As a rain-bow grew a - round the sun, all my stars I loved __ who died __ came from some -

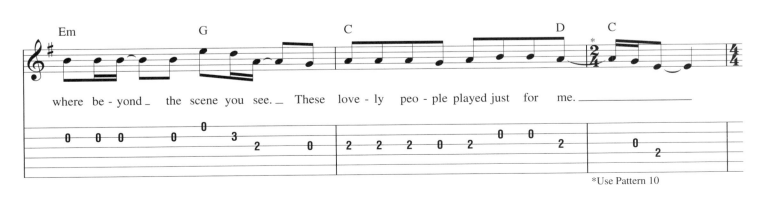

where be - yond __ the scene you see. __ These love - ly peo - ple played just for me. _____

*Use Pattern 10

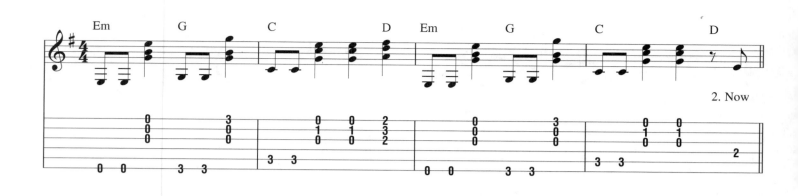

2. Now

Verse

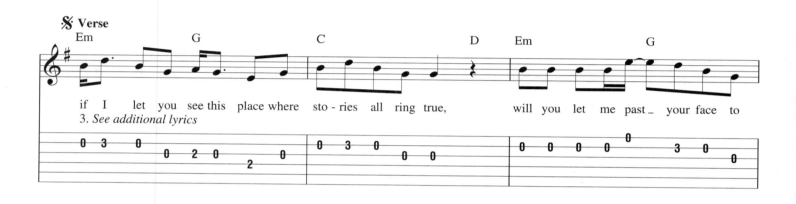

if I   let   you   see this   place where   sto - ries   all   ring   true,   will   you   let   me   past _ your   face   to

3. *See additional lyrics*

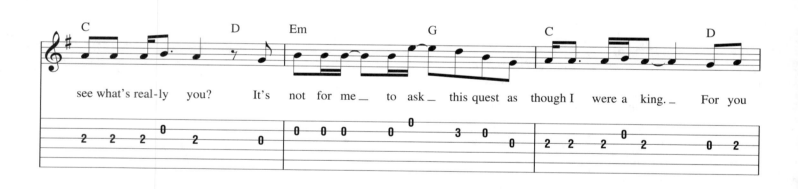

see   what's   real-ly   you?   It's   not   for   me _   to   ask _   this quest   as   though I   were   a   king. _   For you

have   to   love, _   be - lieve, _   and feel _   be - fore _   the   burst _   of   tam - bou - rines _____

34

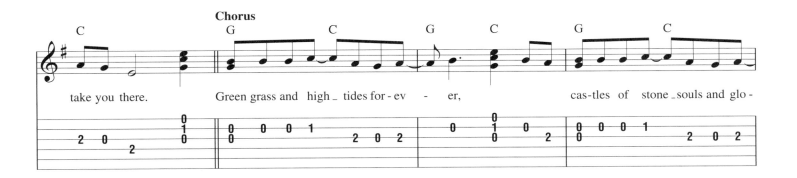

take you there.   Green grass and high _ tides for - ev - er,   cas-tles of   stone _ souls and glo-

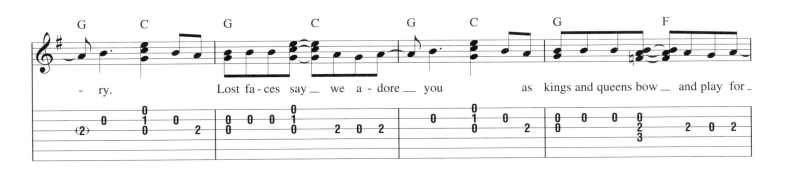

- ry.   Lost fa - ces say _ we a - dore _ you   as   kings and queens bow _ and play for _

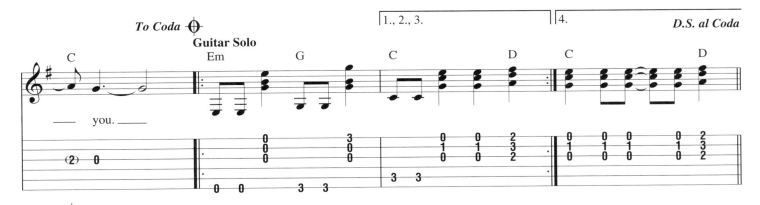

— you. —

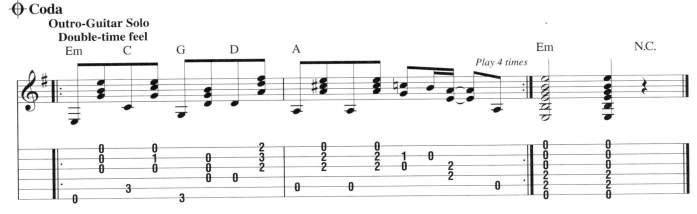

Additional Lyrics

3. Those who don't believe me
   Find your souls and set them free.
   Those who do, believe and love
   As time will be your key.
   Time and time again I've thanked them
   For a peace of mind.
   They helped me find myself amongst
   The music and the rhyme
   That enchants you there.

Highway Star

Words and Music by Ritchie Blackmore, Ian Gillan, Roger Glover, Jon Lord and Ian Paice

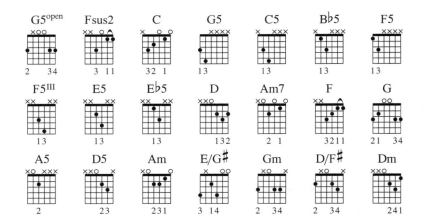

Strum Pattern: 1
Pick Pattern: 2

Intro
Fast Rock

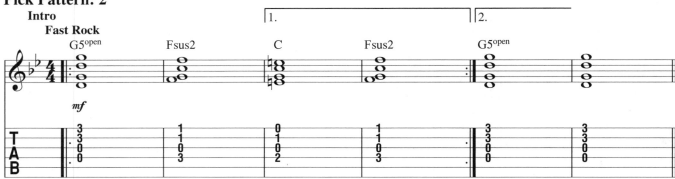

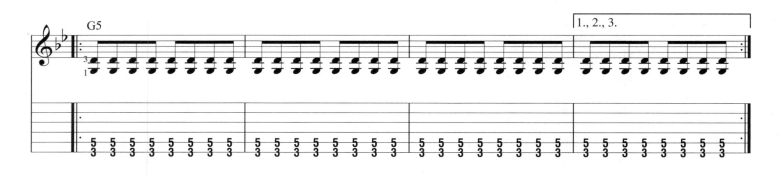

I'm So Sick

**Words and Music by Sameer Bhattacharya, Jared Hartmann,
Kirkpatrick Seals, James Culpepper and Lacey Mosley**

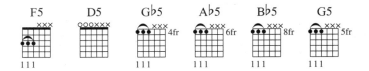

*Drop D tuning:
(low to high) D-A-D-G-B-E

Strum Pattern: 3
Pick Pattern: 3

Intro
Moderate Rock

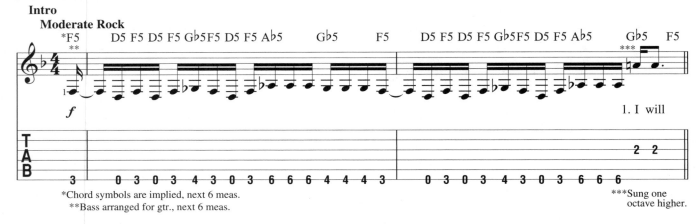

1. I will

*Chord symbols are implied, next 6 meas.
**Bass arranged for gtr., next 6 meas.

***Sung one
octave higher.

Verse

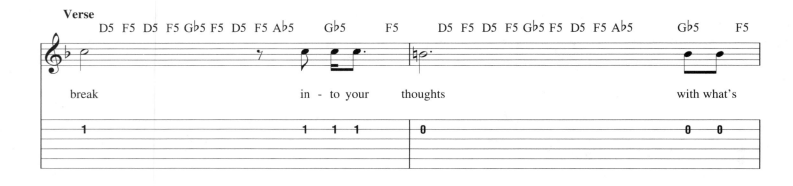

break   in - to your   thoughts   with what's

writ - ten   on   my   heart.   I will

†Gtr.
enters.

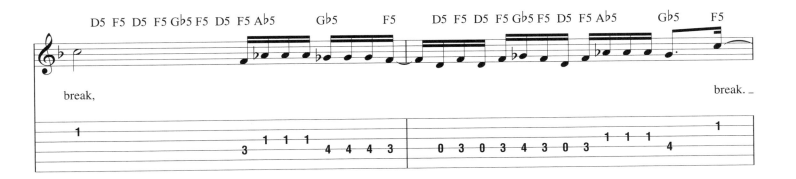

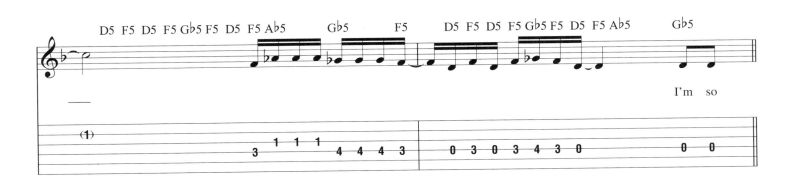

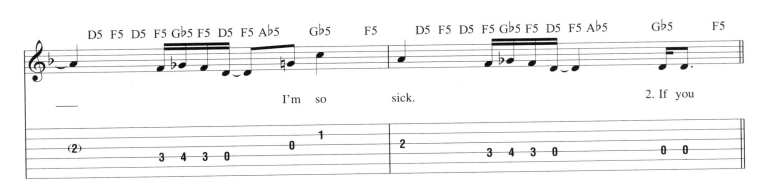

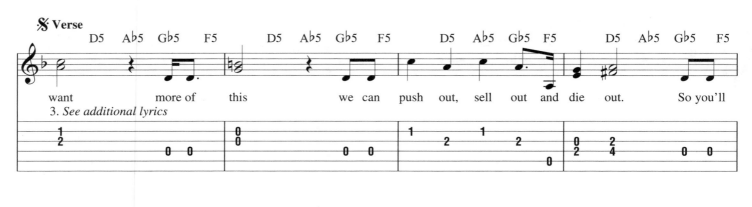

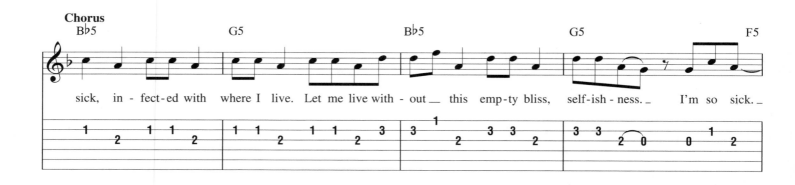

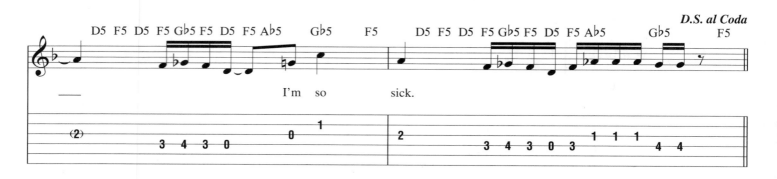

Chorus

sick, in-fect-ed with where I live. Let me live with-out __ this emp-ty bliss, self-ish-ness. __ I'm so, __

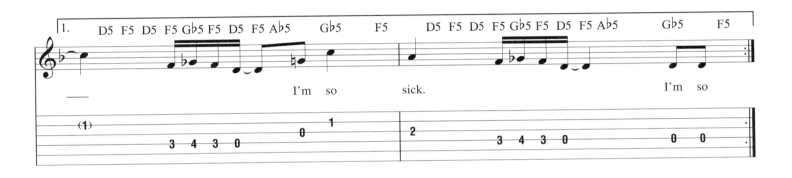

I'm so sick. I'm so

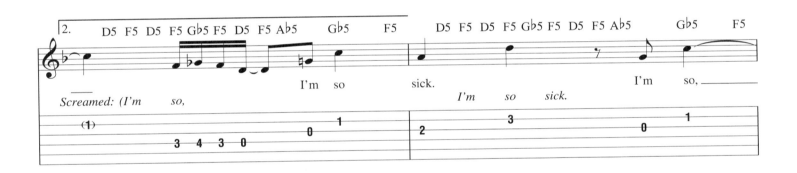

Screamed: (I'm so, I'm so sick. I'm so, __

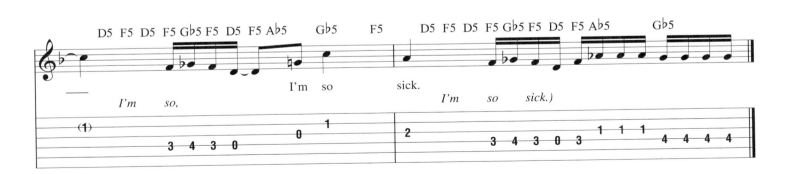

I'm so, I'm so sick. I'm so sick.)

Additional Lyrics

2. Hear it. I'm screaming it.
   You're heading to it now.
   Hear it. I'm screaming it.
   You tremble at this sound.

In Bloom

Words and Music by Kurt Cobain

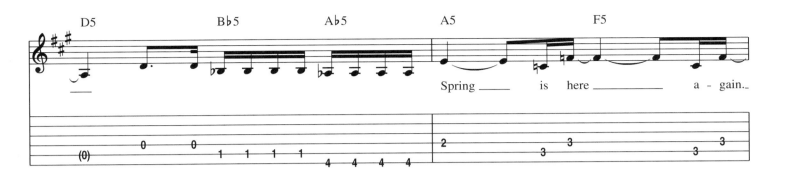

𝄋 Chorus

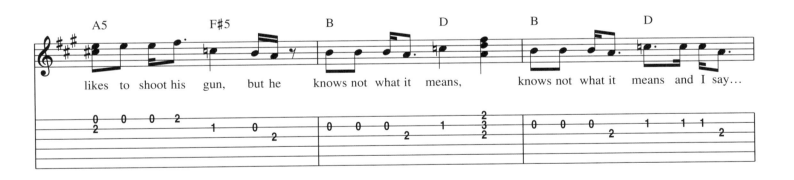

Additional Lyrics

2. We can have some more.
   Nature is a whore.
   Bruises on the fruit.
   Tender age in bloom.

Maps

Words and Music by Karen Orzolek, Nick Zinner and Brian Chase

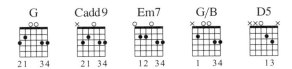

Strum Pattern: 1
Pick Pattern: 1

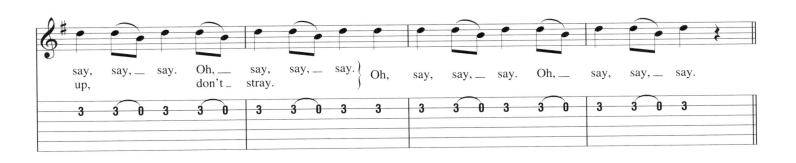

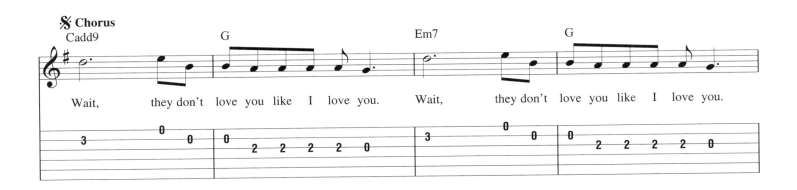

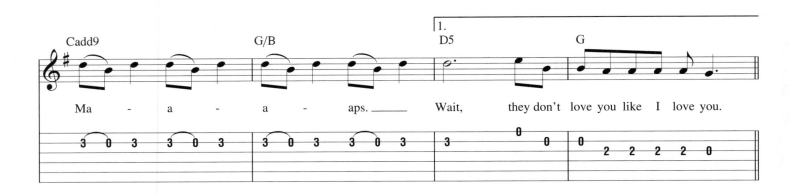

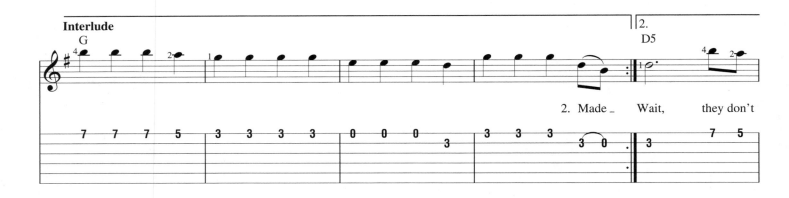

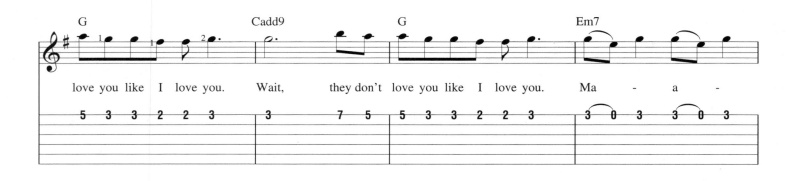

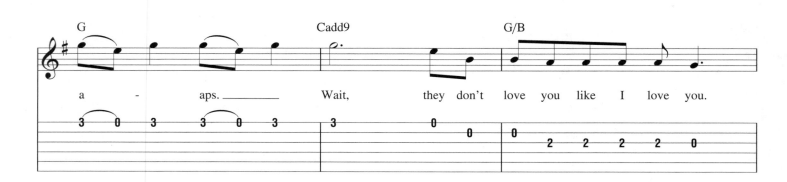

Interlude

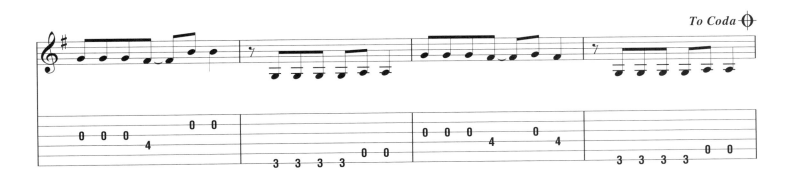

To Coda ⊕

D.S. al Coda
(take 2nd ending)

⊕ **Coda**

Learn to Fly

Words and Music by Dave Grohl, Nate Mendel and Taylor Hawkins

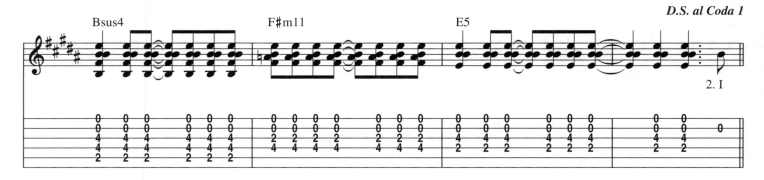

Coda 1

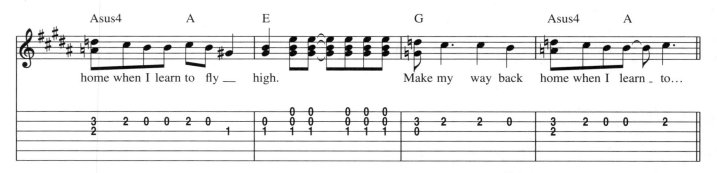

Bridge

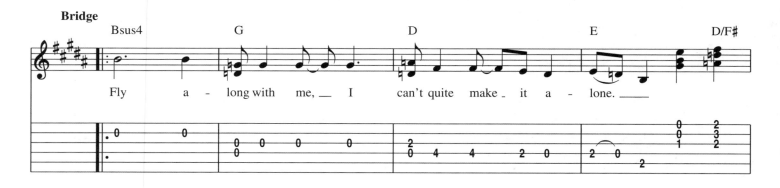

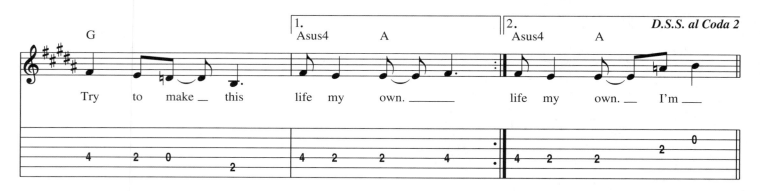

Coda 2

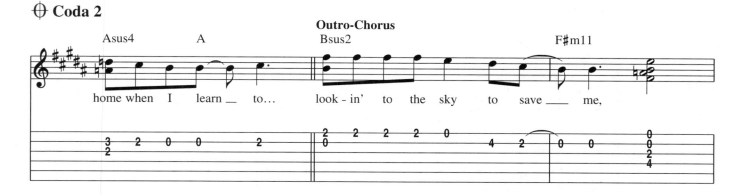

Additional Lyrics

2. I think I'm dyin' missing patience,
   It can wait one night.
   Give it all away if you give me one last try.
   We'll live happily ever trapped
   If you just save my life.
   Runnin' down the angels and ev'rything's all right.

Long Time

Words and Music by Tom Scholz

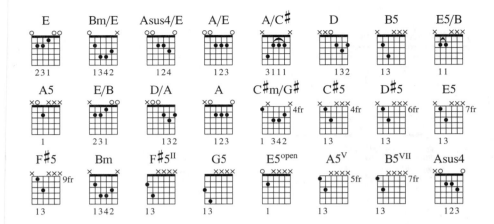

*Capo I

Strum Pattern: 5
Pick Pattern: 3

Intro

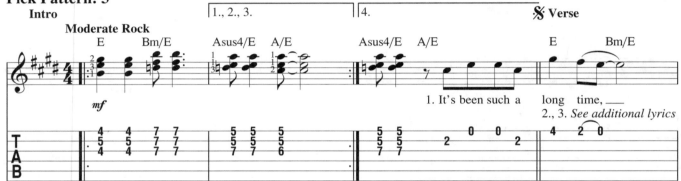

1. It's been such a long time,___
2., 3. *See additional lyrics*

*Optional: To match recording, place capo at first fret.

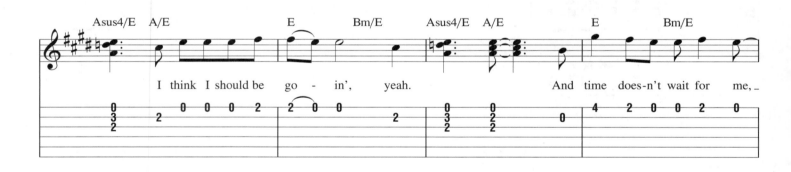

I think I should be go - in', yeah. And time does-n't wait for me,___

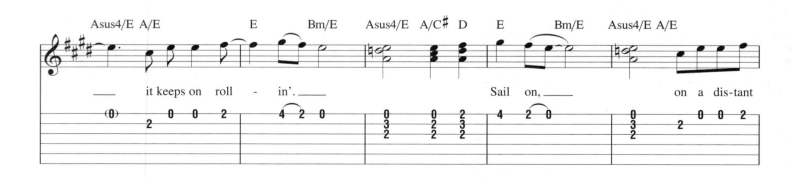

___ it keeps on roll - in'.___ Sail on,___ on a dis-tant

high-way, ___ yeah. ___ I've got to keep on ___ chas-in' a dream, _ I've got-ta be on

my ___ way. ___ Wish there was some-thing I could say. ___

*Strum muted strings.

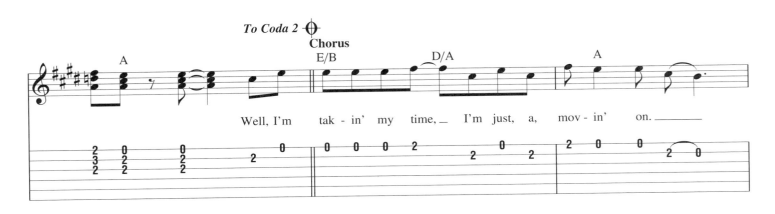

Well, I'm tak-in' my time, ___ I'm just, a, mov-in' on. ___

You'll for-get a-bout me af-ter I've been gone.__ And I take what I find.__ I don't__

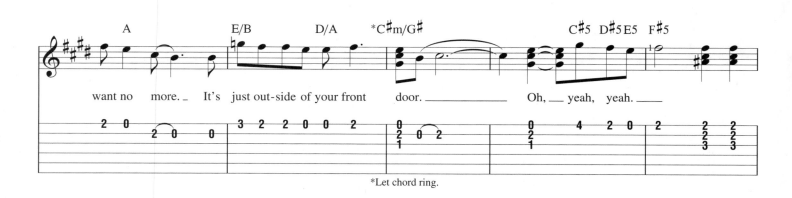

want no more.__ It's just out-side of your front door._____ Oh, __ yeah, yeah. __

*Let chord ring.

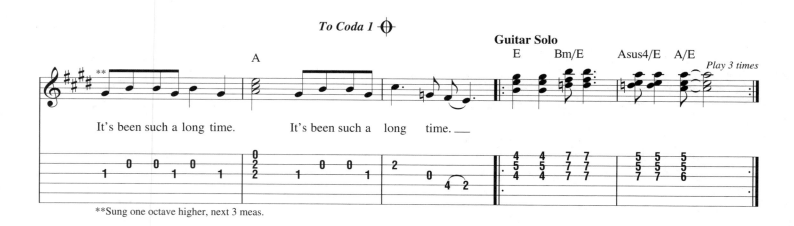

To Coda 1 ⊕

Guitar Solo

Play 3 times

It's been such a long time. It's been such a long time. __

**Sung one octave higher, next 3 meas.

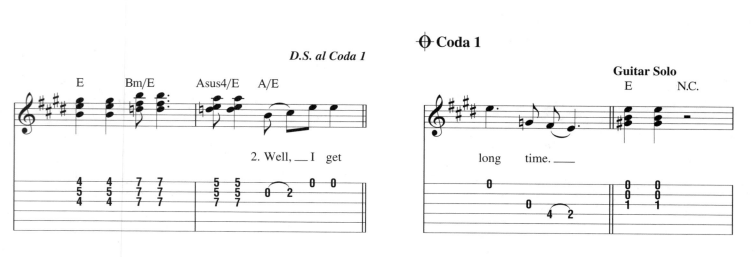

⊕ **Coda 1**

D.S. al Coda 1

Guitar Solo

2. Well, __ I get

long time. __

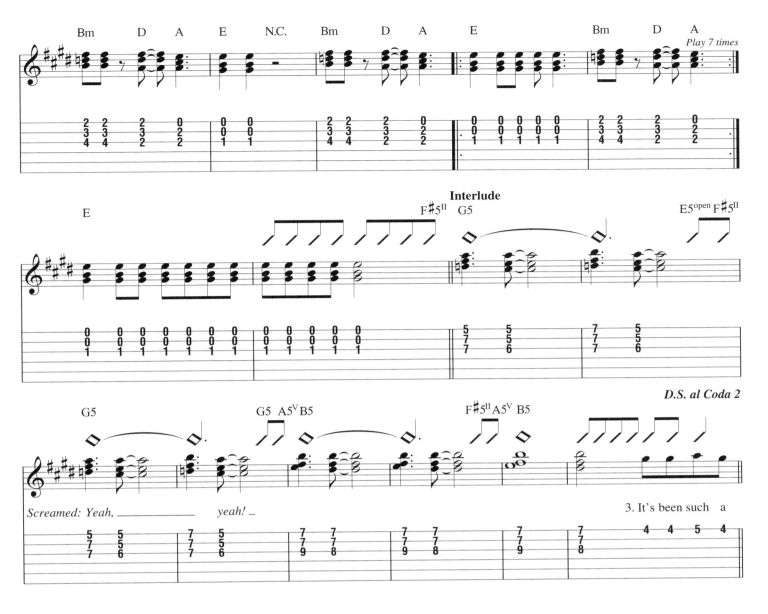

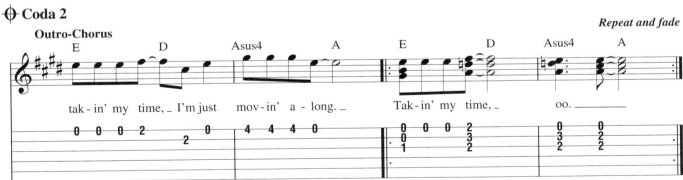

Additional Lyrics

2. Well, I get so lonely when I am without you.
   But in my mind, deep in my mind, I can't forget about you, whoa.
   Good times, and faces that remind me, yeah.
   I'm tryin' to forget your name and leave it all behind me.
   You're comin' back to find me.

3. It's been such a long time, I think I should be goin', yeah.
   And time doesn't wait for me, it keeps on rollin'.
   There's a long road I gotta stay in time with, yeah.
   I've got to keep on chasin' that dream, though I may never find it.
   I'm always just behind it.

Mississippi Queen

Words and Music by Leslie West, Felix Pappalardi, Corky Laing and David Rea

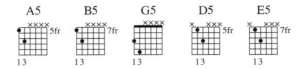

Strum Pattern: 4
Pick Pattern: 3

Intro
Moderately

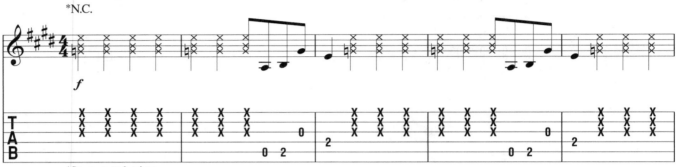

*Strum muted strings.

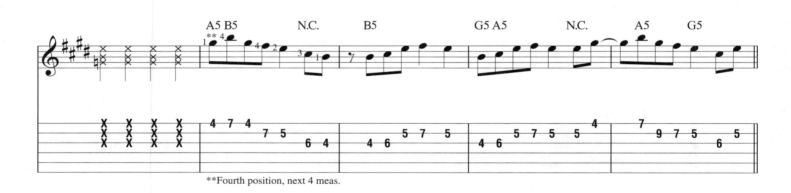

**Fourth position, next 4 meas.

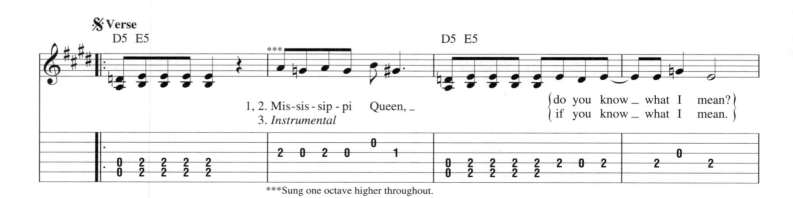

1, 2. Mis-sis-sip-pi Queen, _

3. *Instrumental*

{ do you know _ what I mean? }
{ if you know _ what I mean. }

***Sung one octave higher throughout.

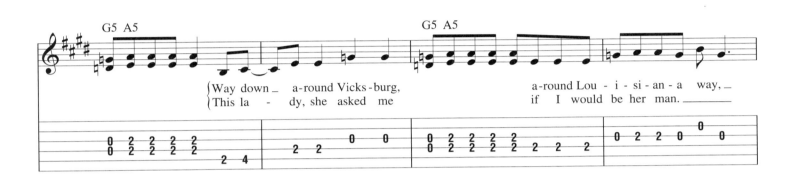

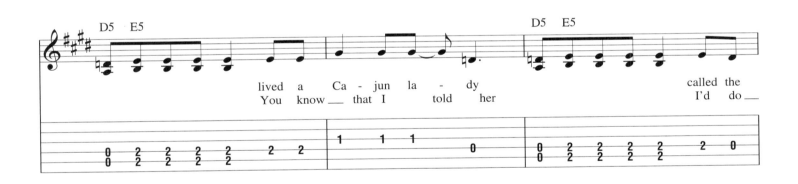

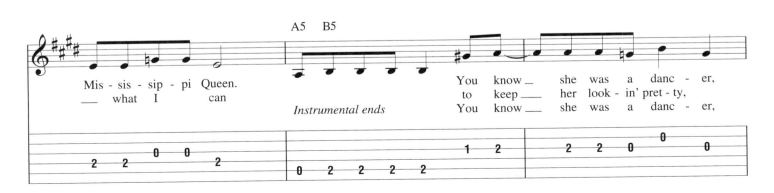

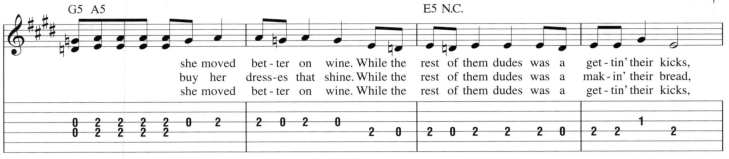

she moved bet - ter on wine. While the rest of them dudes was a get - tin' their kicks,
buy her dress - es that shine. While the rest of them dudes was a mak - in' their bread,
she moved bet - ter on wine. While the rest of them dudes was a get - tin' their kicks,

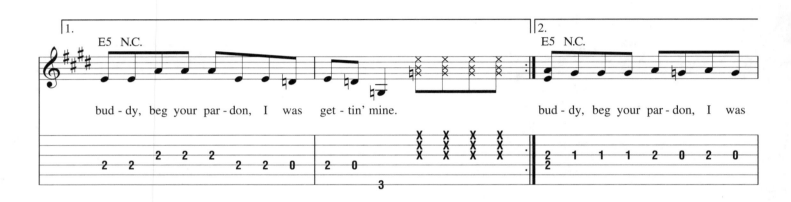

bud - dy, beg your par - don, I was get - tin' mine.

bud - dy, beg your par - don, I was

Coda

D.S. al Coda

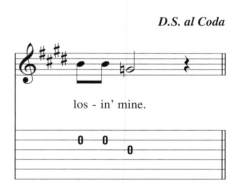

los - in' mine.

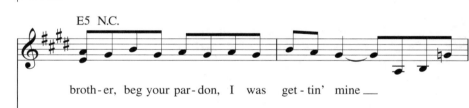

broth - er, beg your par - don, I was get - tin' mine ___

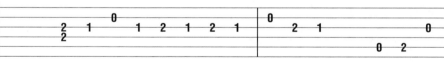

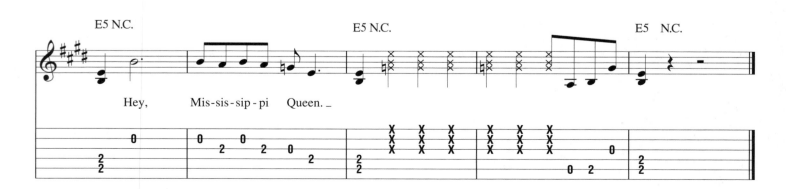

Hey, Mis - sis - sip - pi Queen. ___

Paranoid

Words and Music by Anthony Iommi, John Osbourne, William Ward and Terence Butler

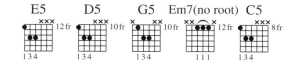

Strum Pattern: 1

Interlude

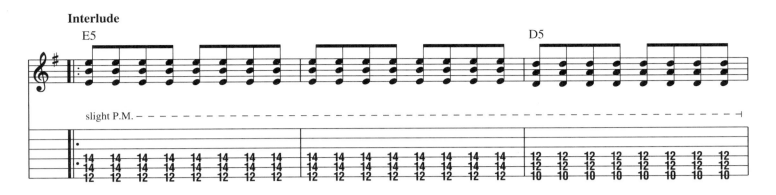

Verse

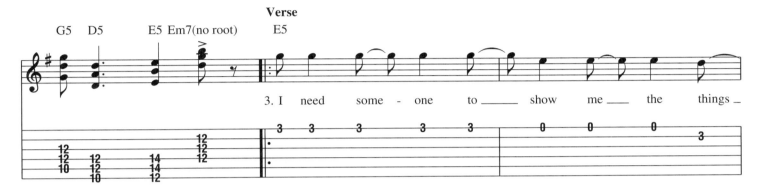

3. I need some - one to _____ show me _____ the things _____

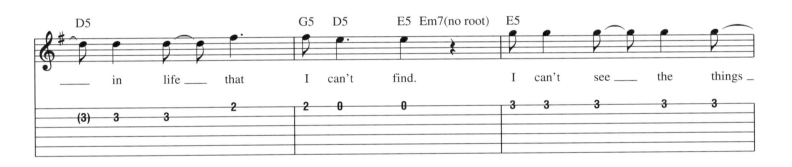

_____ in life _____ that I can't find. I can't see _____ the things _____

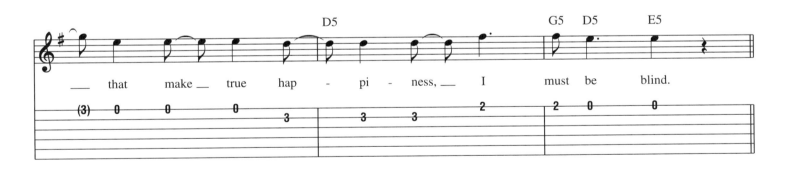

_____ that make _____ true hap - pi - ness, _____ I must be blind.

Guitar Solo

Interlude

⊕ Coda

2nd time, D.S. al Coda

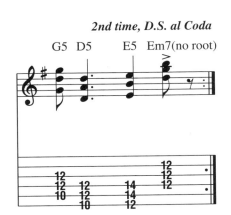

Outro

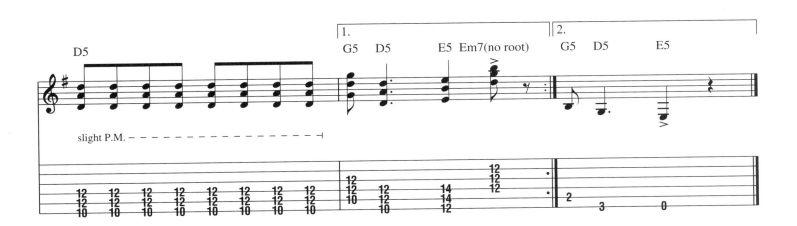

Additional Lyrics

4. Make a joke and I will sigh
   And you will laugh and I will cry.
   Happiness I cannot feel
   And love to me is so unreal.

5. And so as you hear these words
   Telling you now of my state.
   I tell you to enjoy life,
   I wish I could but it's too late.

Next to You

Music and Lyrics by Sting

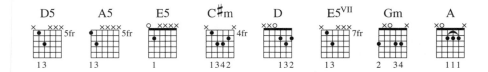

Strum Pattern: 1
Pick Pattern: 2

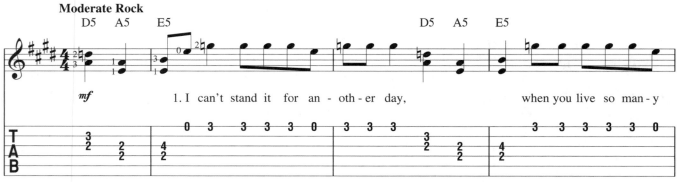

1. I can't stand it for an-oth-er day, when you live so man-y miles a-way.

Noth-in' here is gon-na make me stay. You took me o-ver, let me

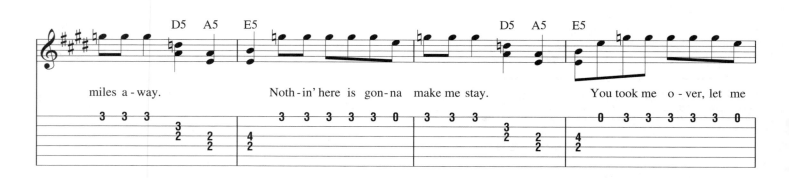

find a way.

2. I sold my house, I sold my mo-tor too. All I want is to be
3. I've had a thou-sand girls or may-be more, but I've nev-er felt like

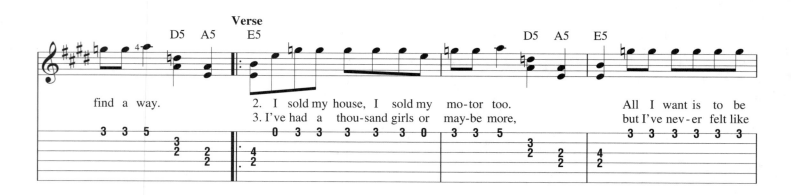

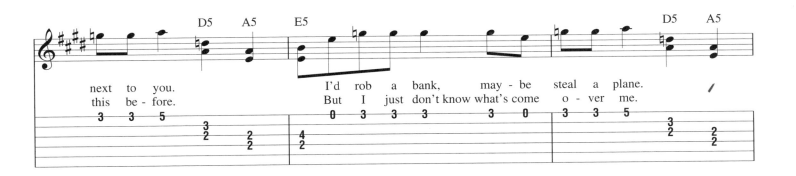

next to you,   all I want is to be next to you,   all I want is to be next to you.

Guitar Solo

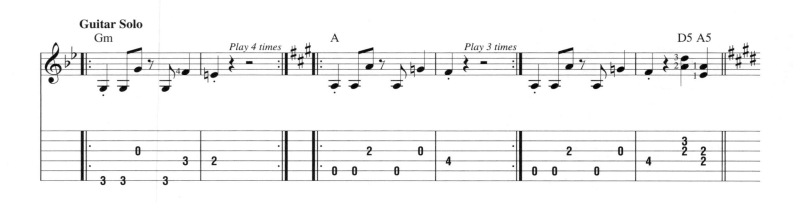

Play 4 times   *Play 3 times*

Verse

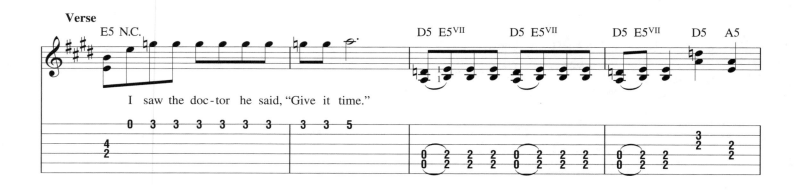

I saw the doc-tor he said, "Give it time."

I've got this feel-in', gon-na   lose my mind.

When all it is, is just a love af - fair.

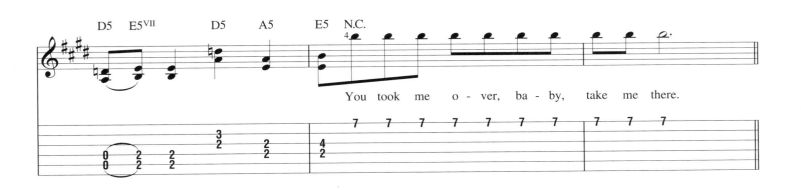

You took me o - ver, ba - by, take me there.

Chorus

What can I do, _____ all I want is to be next to you. _____ next to you.

Repeat and fade

All I want is to be next to you, all I want is to be next to you.

Run to the Hills

Words and Music by Steven Harris

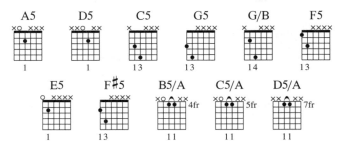

Strum Pattern: 3
Pick Pattern: 3

Intro
Moderate Rock

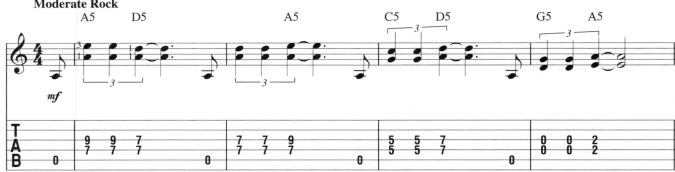

Verse

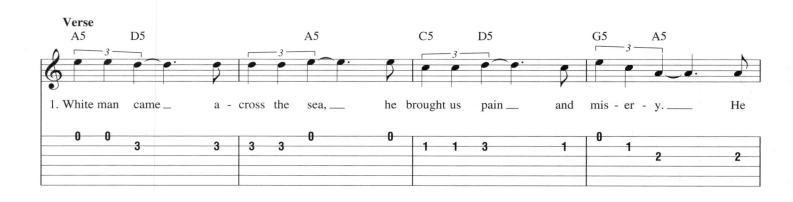

1. White man came ___ a - cross the sea, ___ he brought us pain ___ and mis - er - y. ___ He

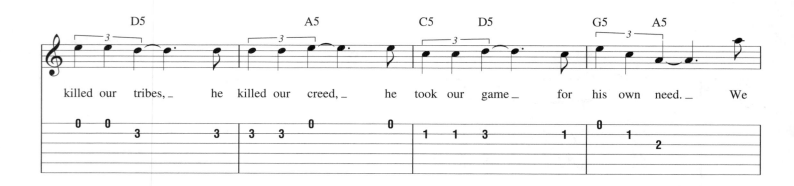

killed our tribes, _ he killed our creed, _ he took our game _ for his own need. _ We

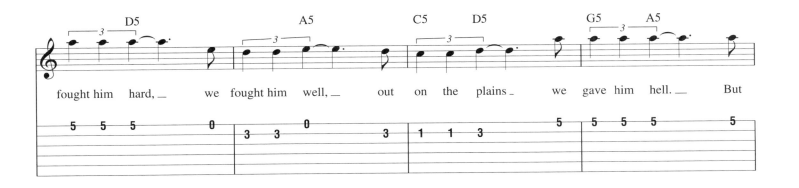

fought him hard, __ we fought him well, __ out on the plains __ we gave him hell. __ But

man - y came, __ too much for Cree. __ Oh, will we ev - er be set free? __

*Let chord ring.

Interlude
Faster

Verse

2. Rid - ing through dust clouds and bar - ren wastes,
3. Sol - dier blue __ in the bar - ren wastes,

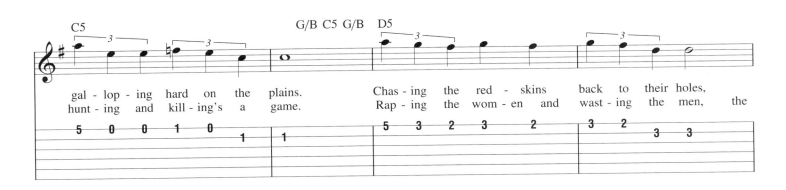

gal - lop - ing hard on the plains. Chas - ing the red - skins back to their holes,
hunt - ing and kill - ing's a game. Rap - ing the wom - en and wast - ing the men, the

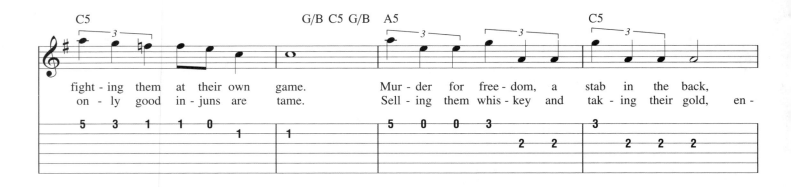

fight - ing them at their own game. Mur - der for free - dom, a stab in the back,
on - ly good in - juns are tame. Sell - ing them whis - key and tak - ing their gold, en -

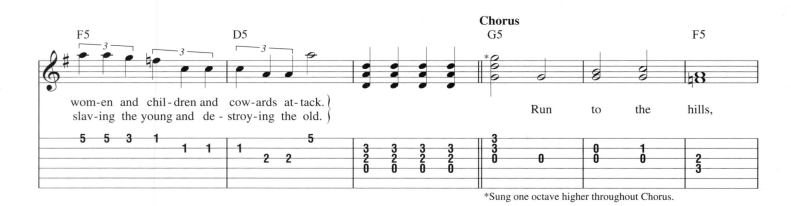

wom-en and chil-dren and cow-ards at-tack.
slav-ing the young and de - stroy-ing the old.

Run to the hills,

*Sung one octave higher throughout Chorus.

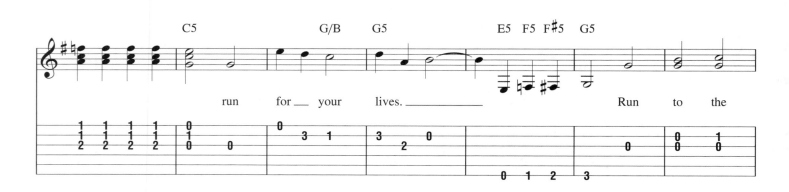

run for __ your lives. _____ Run to the

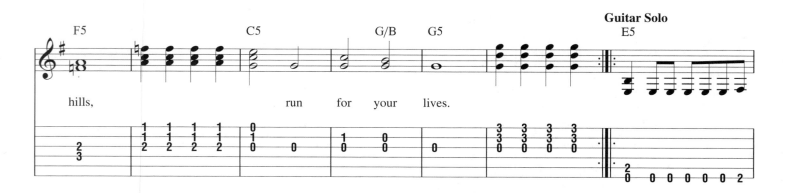

hills, run for your lives.

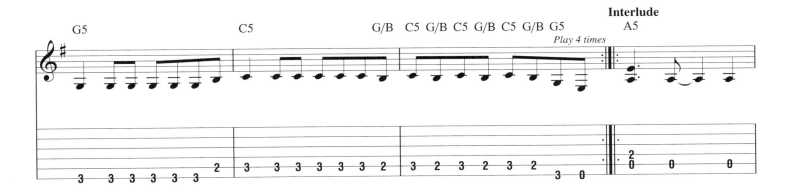

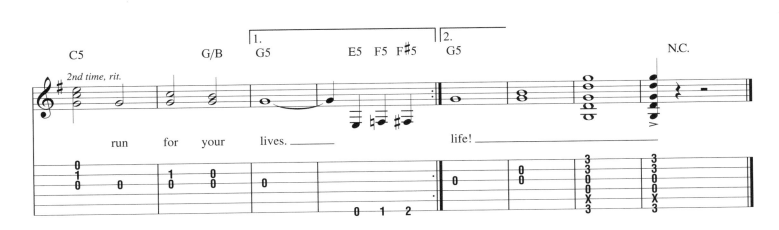

Say It Ain't So

Words and Music by Rivers Cuomo

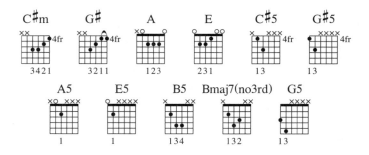

*Tune down 1/2 step:
(low to high) E♭-A♭-D♭-G♭-B♭-E♭

Strum Pattern: 2
Pick Pattern: 4

Intro
Slowly

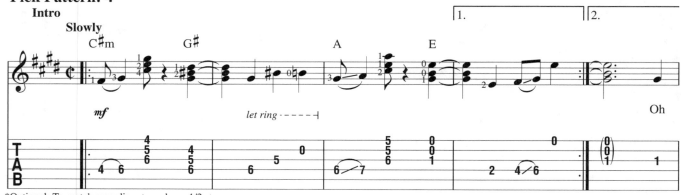

*Optional: To match recording, tune down 1/2 step.

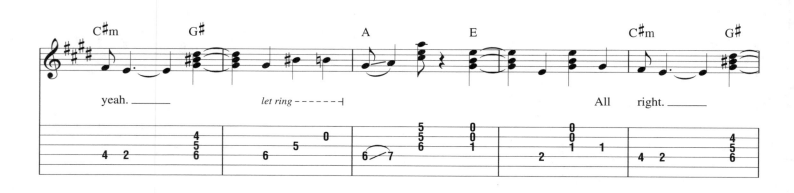

Verse

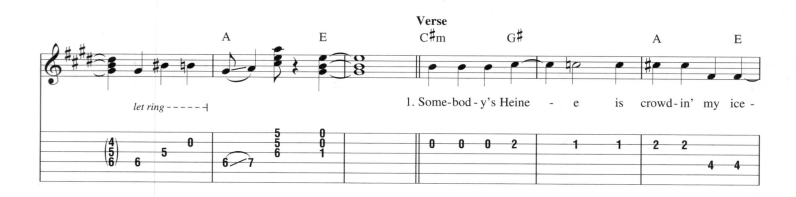

- box. Some-bod-y's cold ____ one is giv-in' me chills. ____ Guess I'll just close ____

____ my eyes. ____ Oh yeah. ____ All right. ____

Feels good ____ in - side. ____

*Let chord ring.

Verse

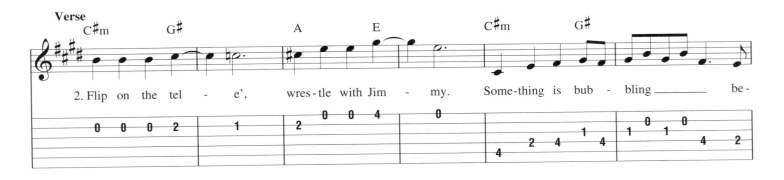

2. Flip on the tel - e', wres-tle with Jim - my. Some-thing is bub - bling ____ be-

hind ____ my back. ____ The bot-tle is read - y to blow. ____

75

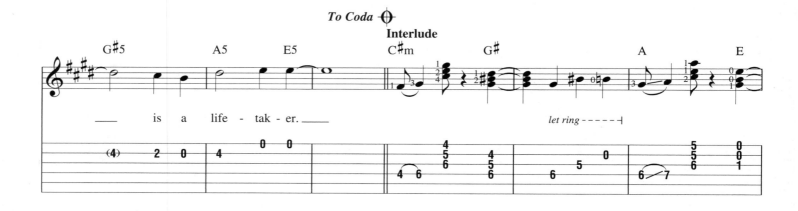

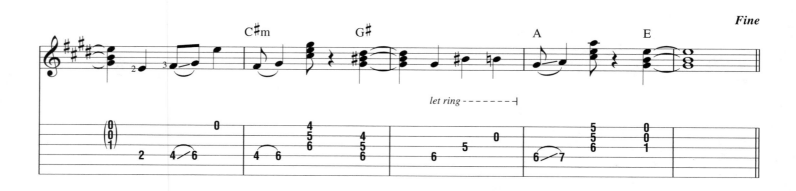

3. I can't con-front___ you. I nev-er could___ do that which might hurt___ you, so

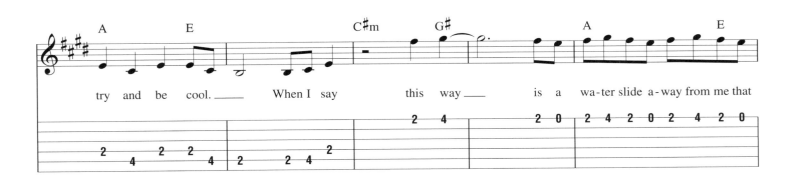

try and be cool.___ When I say this way___ is a wa-ter slide a-way from me that

D.S. al Coda

takes you fur-ther ev-er-y day._____ So be cool.___

Coda
Bridge

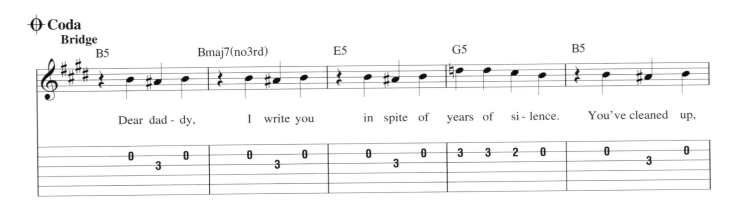

Dear dad-dy, I write you in spite of years of si-lence. You've cleaned up,

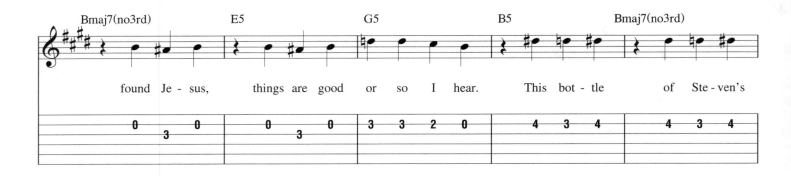

found Je - sus, things are good or so I hear. This bot - tle of Ste - ven's

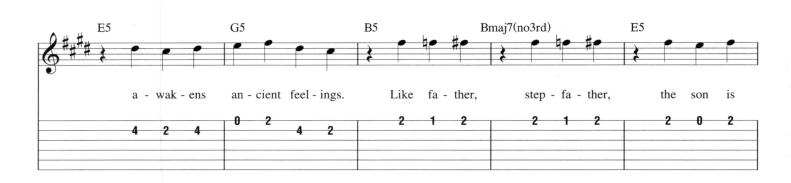

a - wak - ens an - cient feel - ings. Like fa - ther, step - fa - ther, the son is

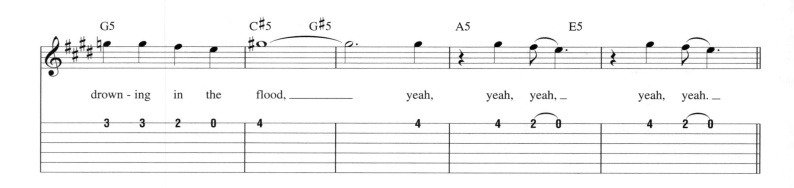

drown - ing in the flood, _____ yeah, yeah, yeah, _ yeah, yeah. _

|1., 2. |2.   ***D.S. al Fine***

Guitar Solo

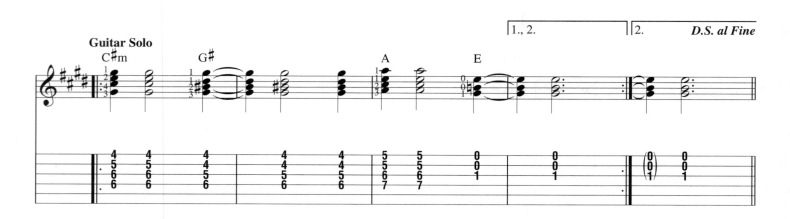

Should I Stay or Should I Go

Words and Music by Mick Jones and Joe Strummer

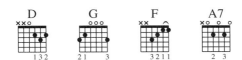

Strum Pattern: 6
Pick Pattern: 5

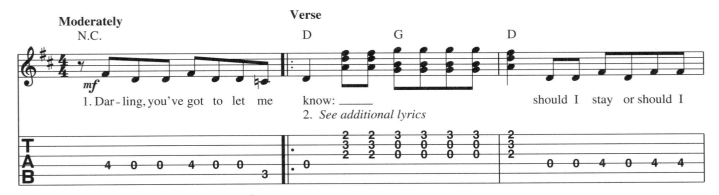

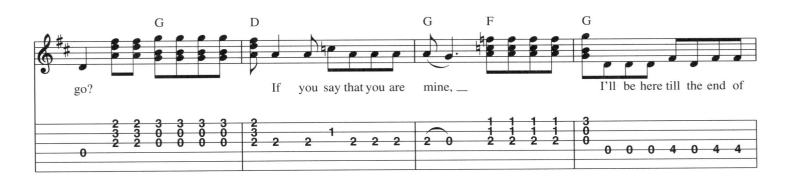

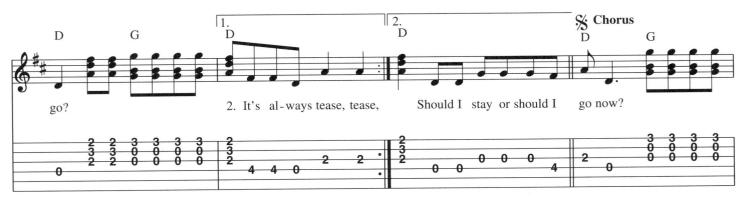

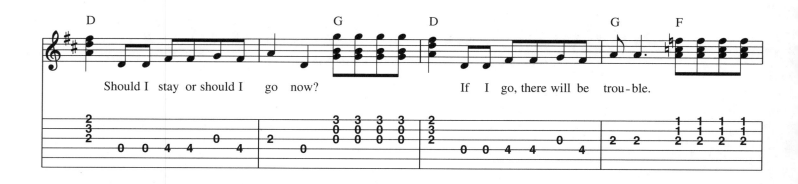

Should I stay or should I go now? If I go, there will be trou-ble.

And if I stay, it will be dou-ble. So you've got to let me know: __

To Coda ⊕

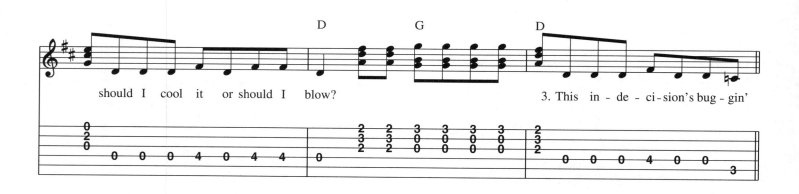

should I cool it or should I blow? 3. This in-de-ci-sion's bug-gin'

Verse

me. If you don't want me set me free. Ex-act-ly who'm I s'posed to

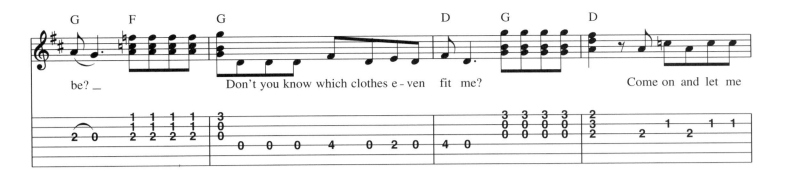

be? — Don't you know which clothes e - ven fit me? Come on and let me

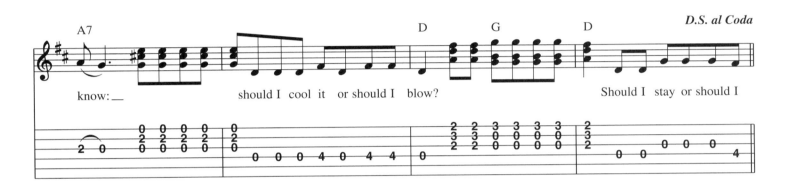

D.S. al Coda

know: — should I cool it or should I blow? Should I stay or should I

⊕ Coda

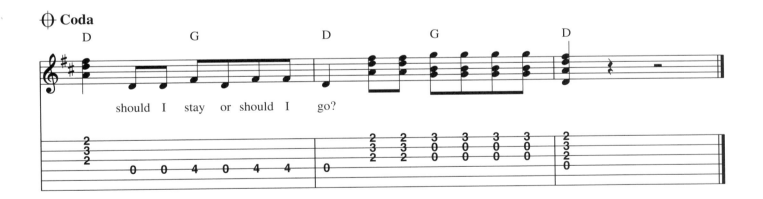

should I stay or should I go?

Additional Lyrics

2. It's always tease, tease, tease.
   You're happy when I'm on my knees.
   One day is fine and next is black.
   So if you want me off your back,
   Well, come on and let me know:
   Should I stay or should I go?

Suffragette City

Words and Music by David Bowie

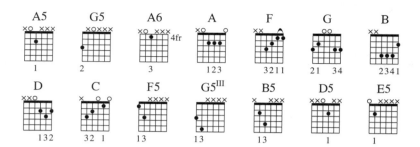

Strum Pattern: 1
Pick Pattern: 1

Intro

Moderate Rock

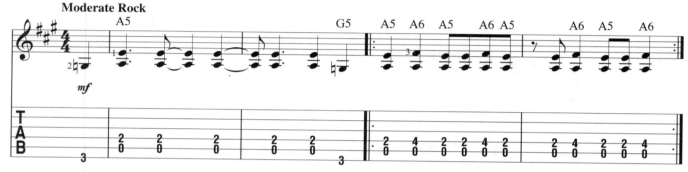

Verse

1. (Hey, man!) Ah, leave me a - lone,_ you know. (Hey, man!) Oh, Hen-ry, get off the phone,_ I got...

(Hey, man!) I got to straight-en my face. _ This mel - low thighed chick_ just put my

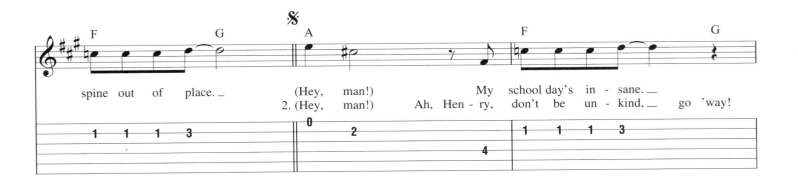

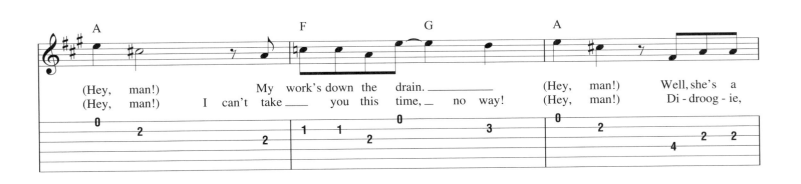

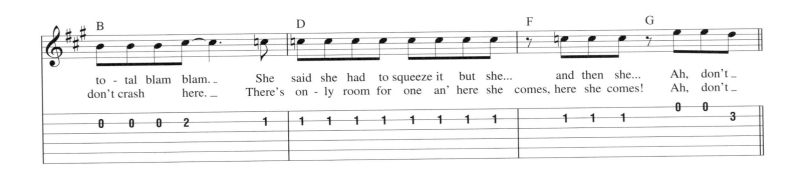

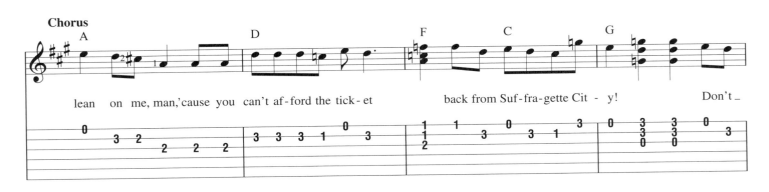

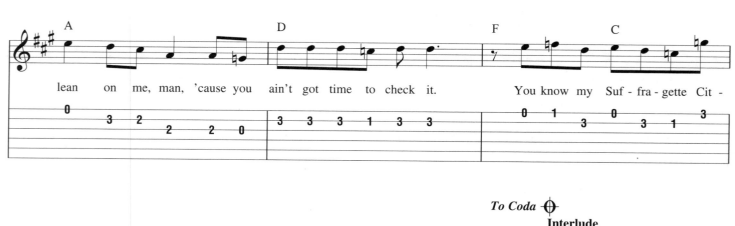

lean on me, man, 'cause you ain't got time to check it. You know my Suf - fra - gette Cit -

y is out - ta sight! She's al - right!

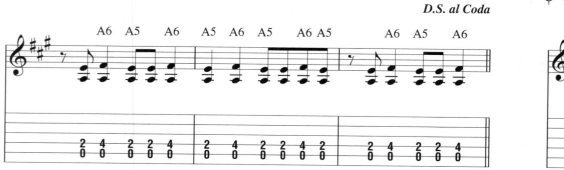

right!

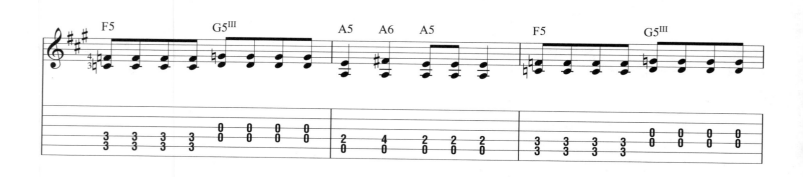

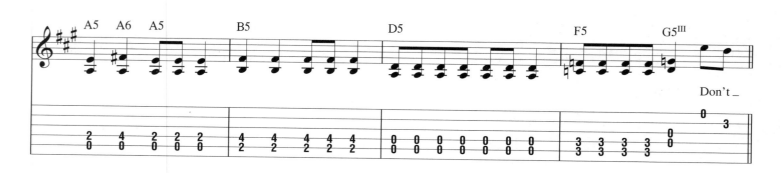

Don't _

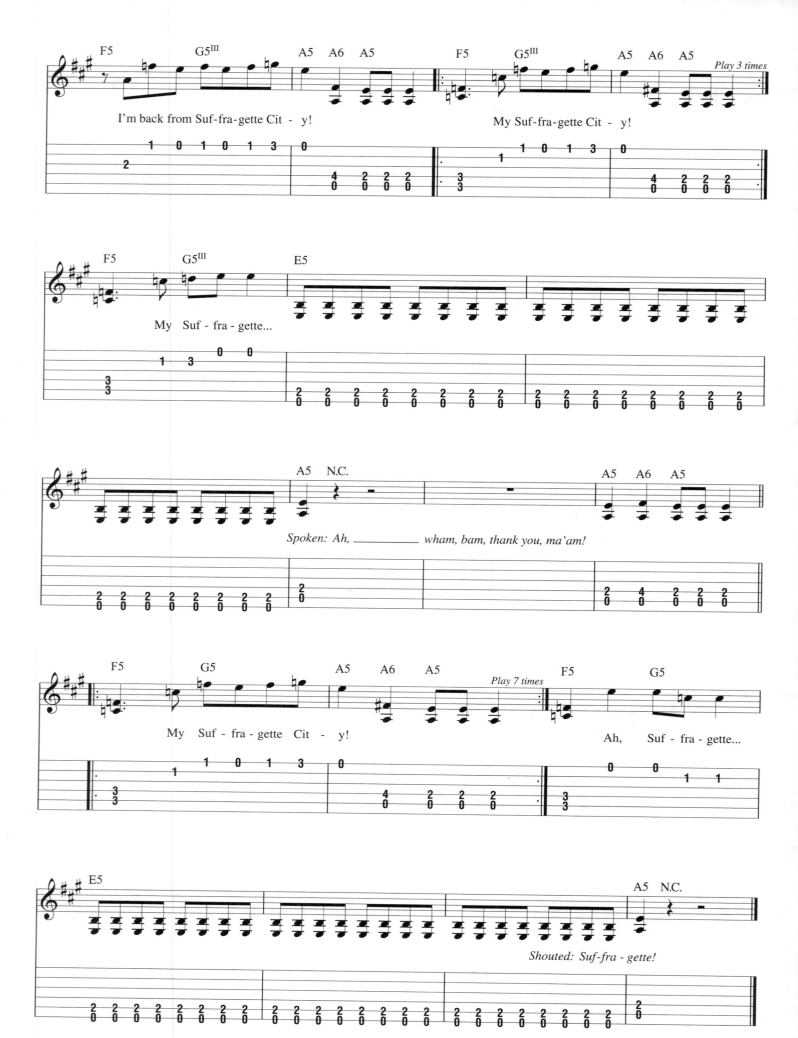

Wanted Dead or Alive

Words and Music by Jon Bon Jovi and Richie Sambora

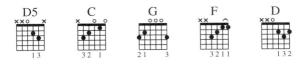

Strum Pattern: 1, 3
Pick Pattern: 2, 4

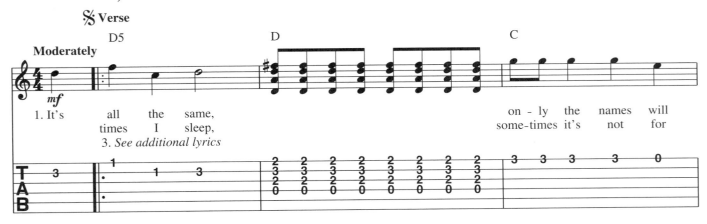

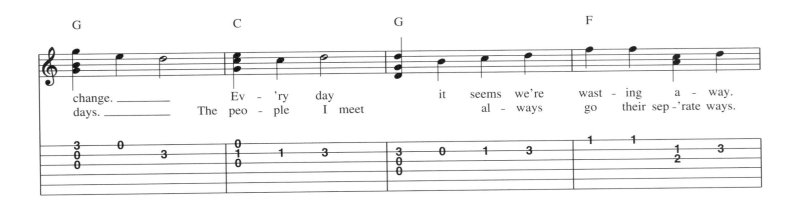

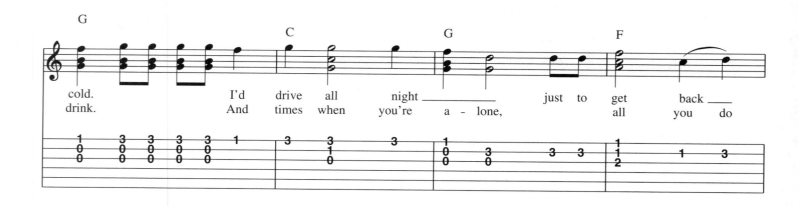

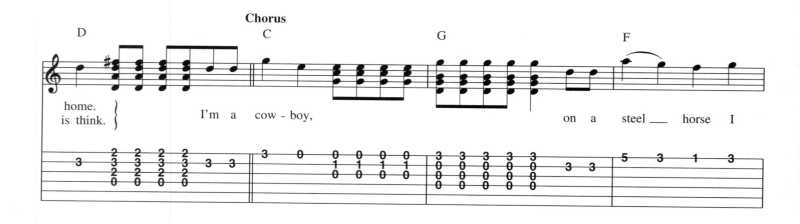

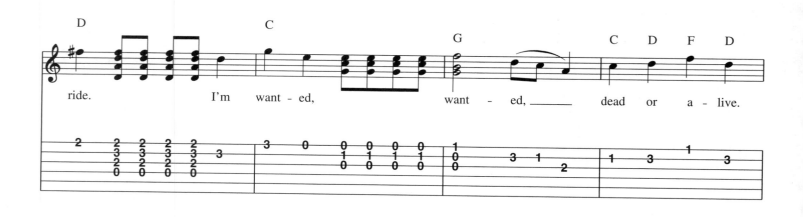

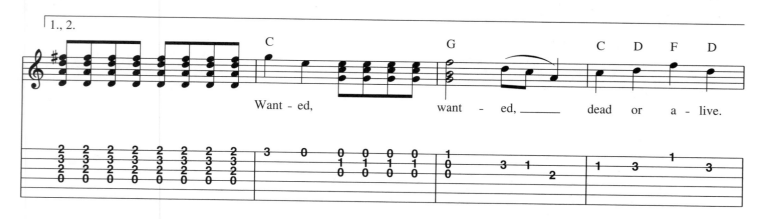

2. Some   'Cause I'm a
3. And I

Outro

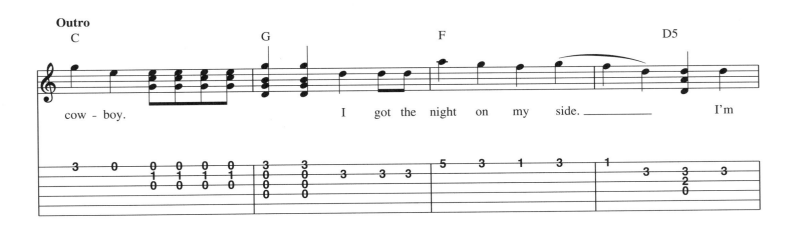

cow - boy.   I   got the night on my side. _____ I'm

want - ed,   want - ed, _____ dead or a - live. _____

Additional Lyrics

3. And I walk these streets,
   A loaded six string on my back.
   I've seen a million faces, and I've rocked them all.
   I've been ev'rywhere, still I'm standing tall.
   I play for keeps, 'cause I might not make it back.

Train Kept A-Rollin'

Words and Music by Tiny Bradshaw, Lois Mann and Howie Kay

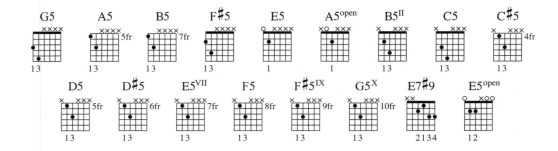

Strum Pattern: 5, 2

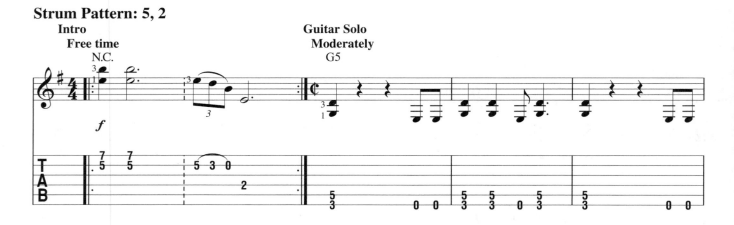

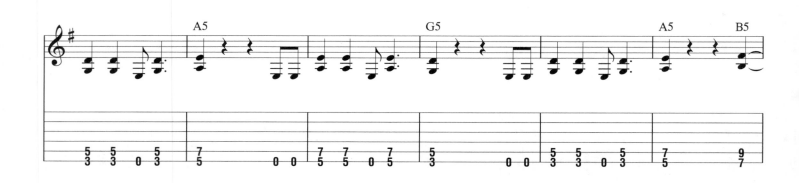

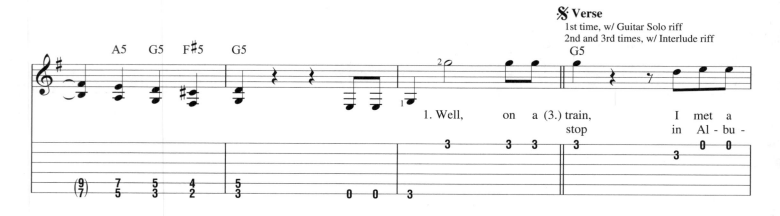

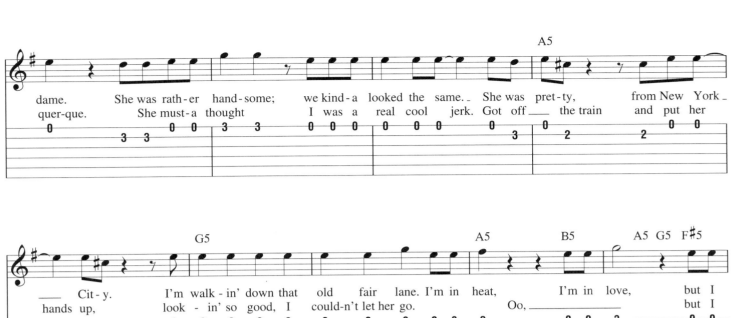

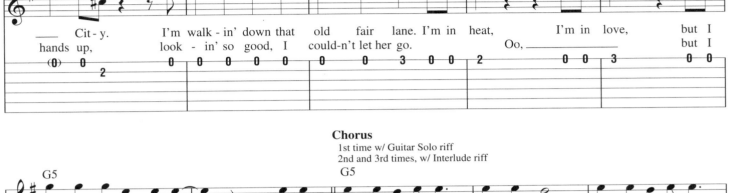

Chorus
1st time w/ Guitar Solo riff
2nd and 3rd times, w/ Interlude riff

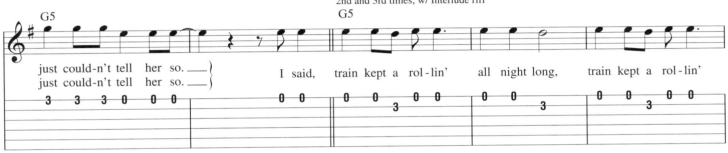

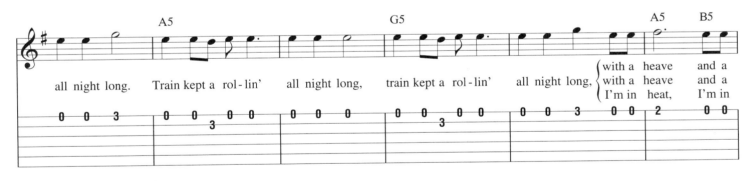

To Coda 1 ⊕
To Coda 2 ⊕

Guitar Solo
w/ Guitar Solo riff

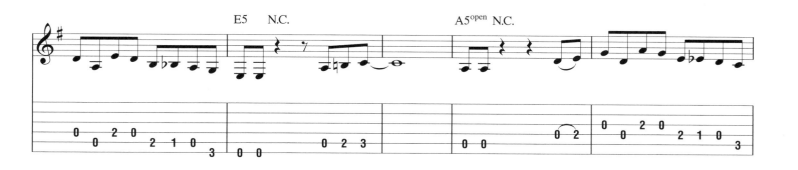

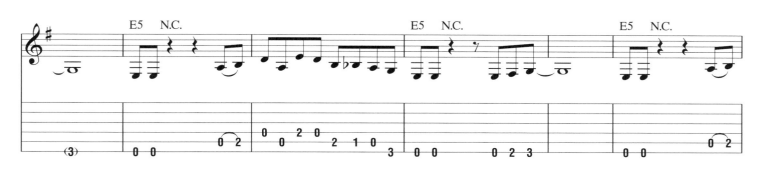

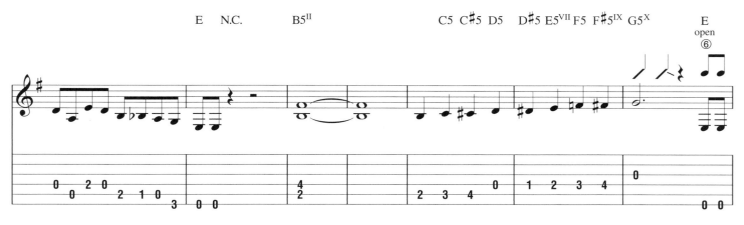

w/ Guitar Solo riff

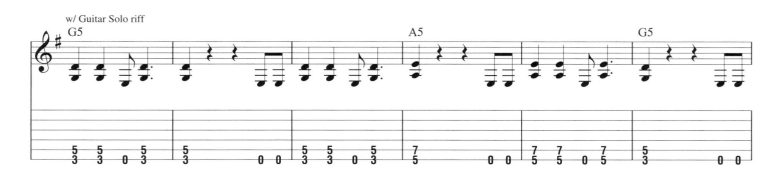

Breakdown

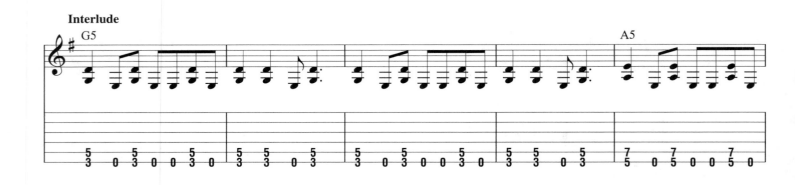

Interlude

D.S. al Coda 1

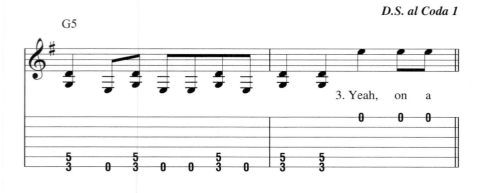

3. Yeah, on a

Coda 1

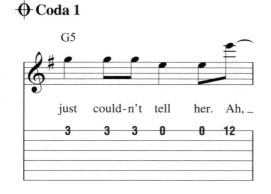

just could-n't tell her. Ah, __

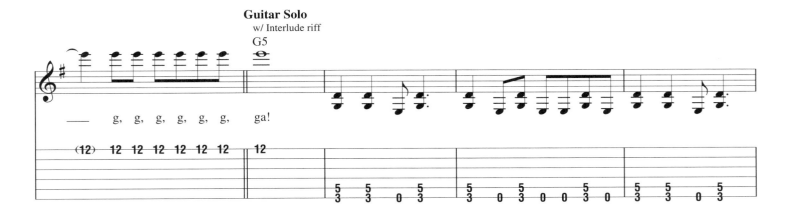

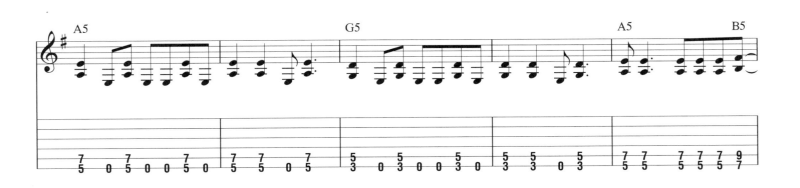

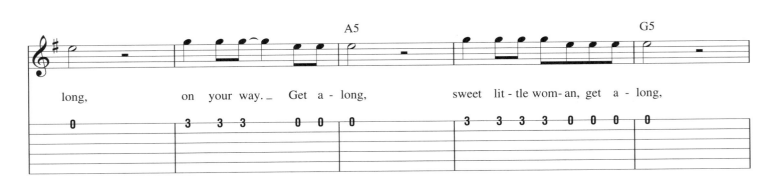

on your way.__ I'm in heat, I'm in love, but I just could-n't tell her, yeah, __ yeah, yeah! __

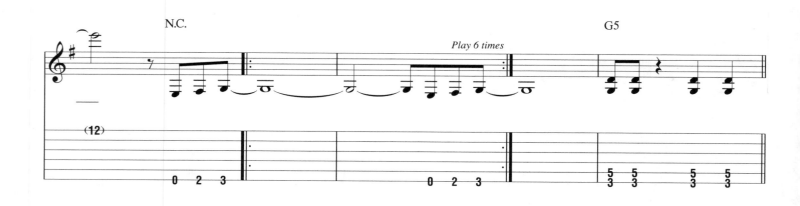

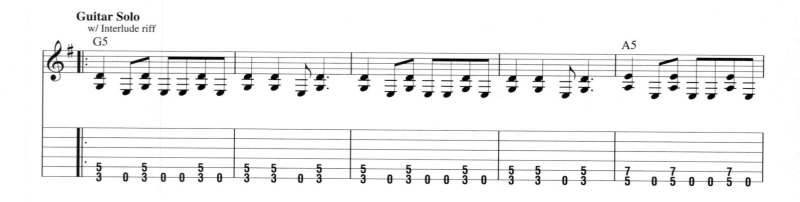

Guitar Solo
w/ Interlude riff

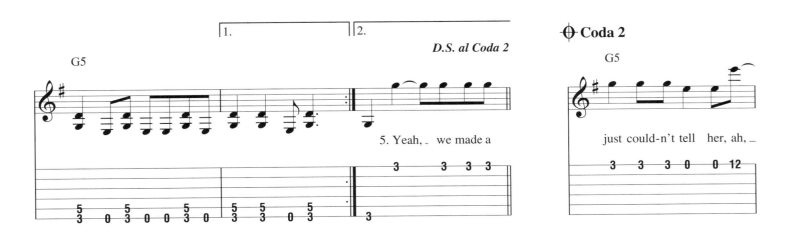

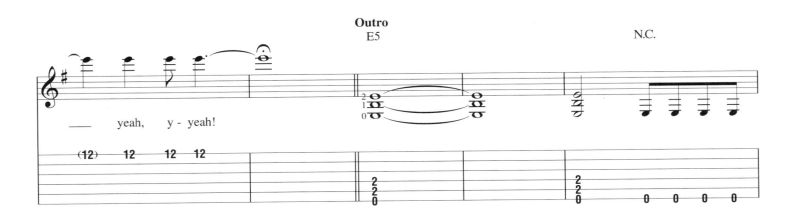

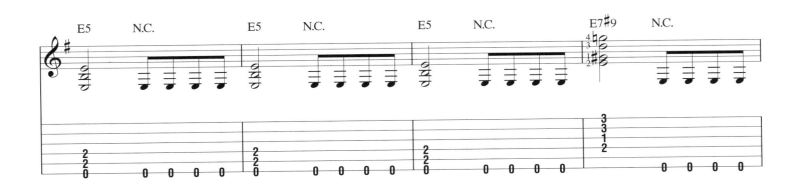

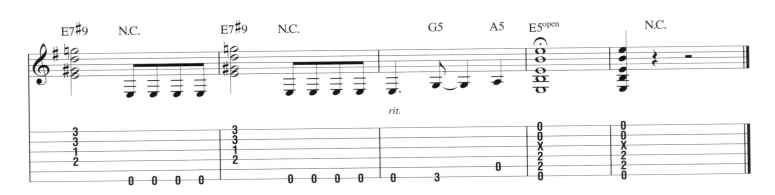

When You Were Young

Words and Music by Brandon Flowers, Dave Keuning, Mark Stoermer and Ronnie Vannucci

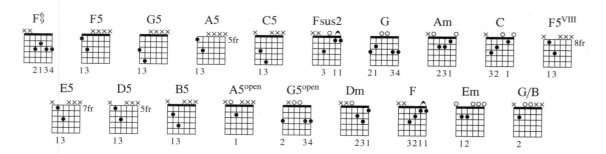

*Tune down 1/2 step:
(low to high) Eb-Ab-Db-Gb-Bb-Eb

Strum Pattern: 1
Pick Pattern: 5

Intro
Moderate Rock

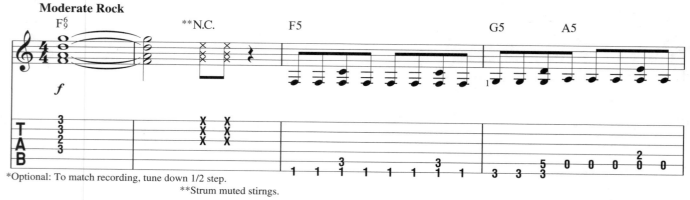

*Optional: To match recording, tune down 1/2 step.
**Strum muted stirngs.

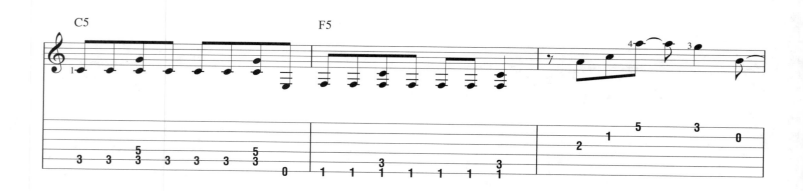

1. You sit there _ in your heart - ache,
2. Can we climb _ this moun-tain? I don't know.

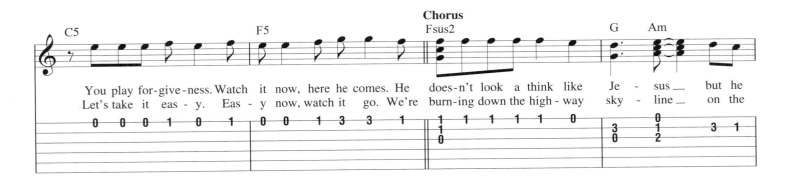

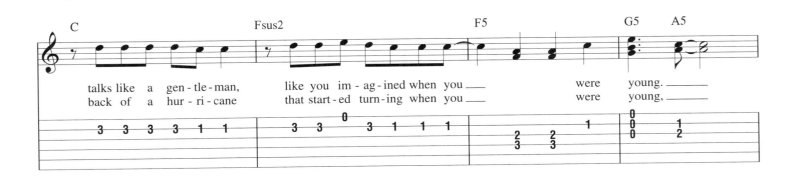

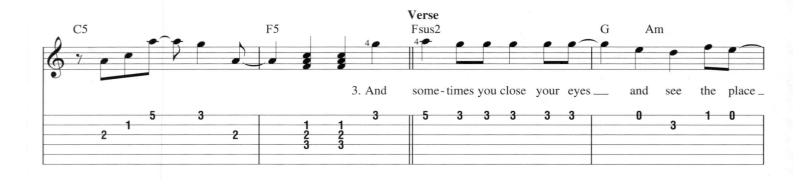

3. And some-times you close your eyes ___ and see the place ___

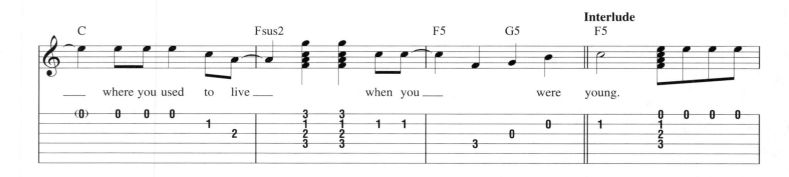

___ where you used to live ___ when you ___ were young.

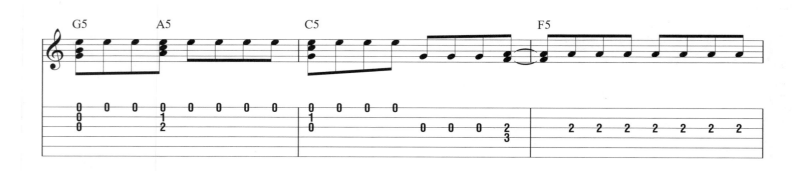

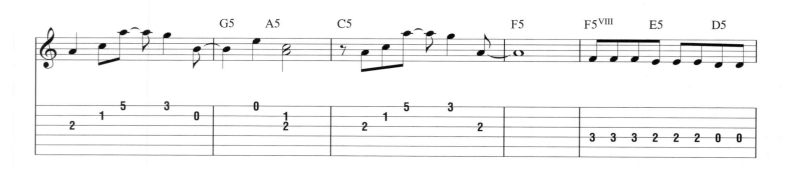

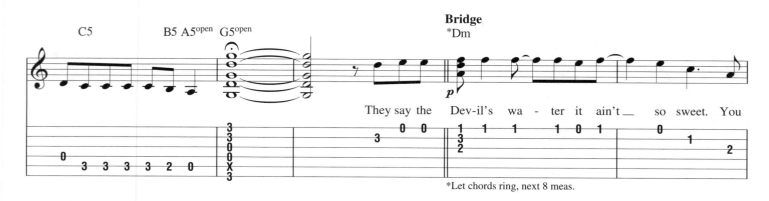

They say the Dev-il's wa - ter it ain't ___ so sweet. You

*Let chords ring, next 8 meas.

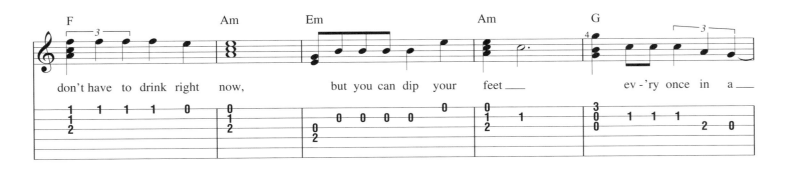

don't have to drink right now, but you can dip your feet ev-'ry once in a

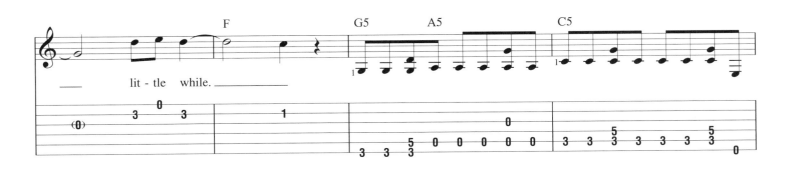

lit - tle while.

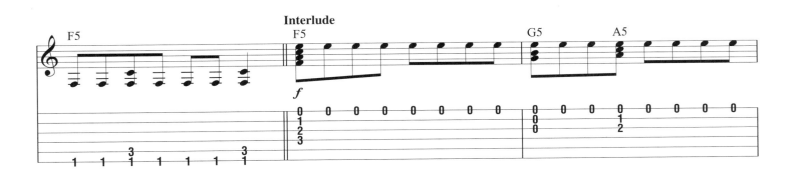

Interlude

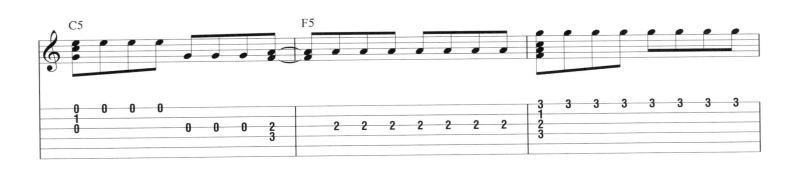

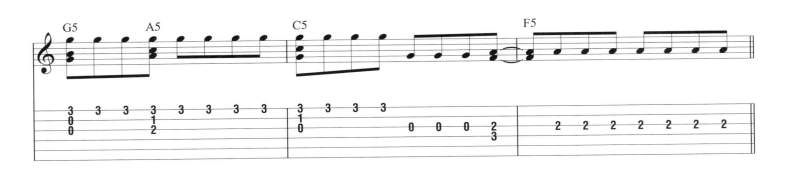

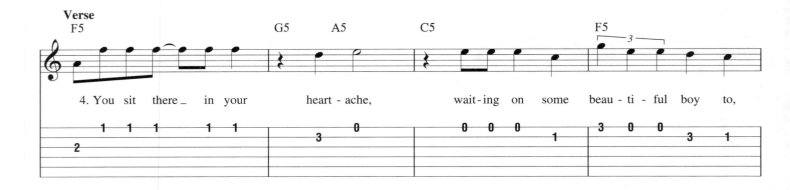

Verse

4. You sit there _ in your heart - ache, wait-ing on some beau - ti - ful boy to,

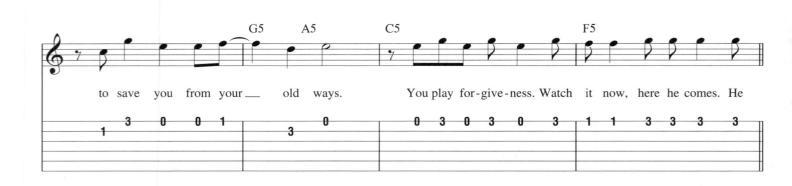

to save you from your ___ old ways. You play for-give-ness. Watch it now, here he comes. He

Outro-Chorus

does - n't look a thing like Je - sus ___ but he talks like a gen - tle - man,

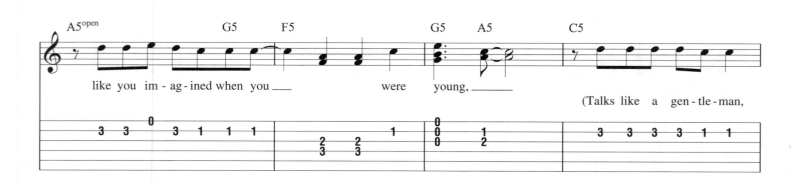

like you im - ag-ined when you ___ were young, _____

(Talks like a gen - tle - man,

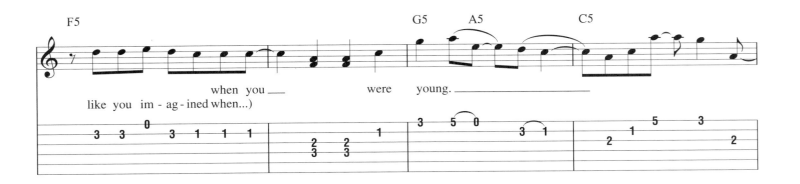

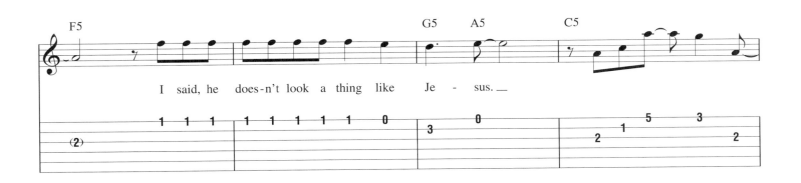

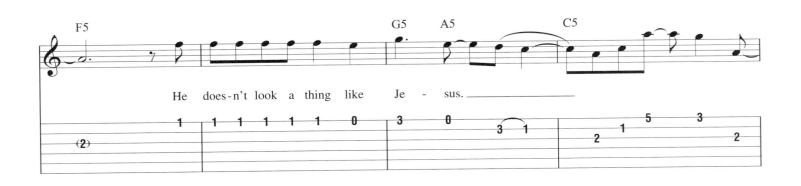

Won't Get Fooled Again

Words and Music by Pete Townshend

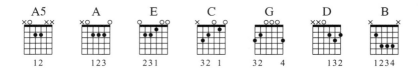

Strum Pattern: 5
Pick Pattern: 1

Intro
Moderately fast

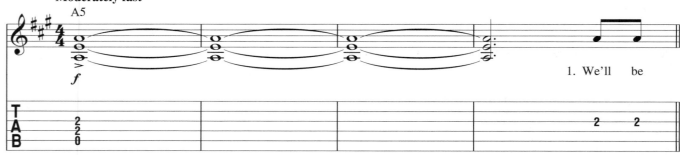

1. We'll be

fight-ing in the streets _ with our chil-dren at our feet, _ and the
2., 3. *See additional lyrics*

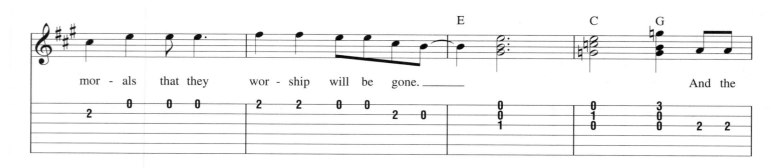

mor-als that they wor-ship will be gone. _ And the

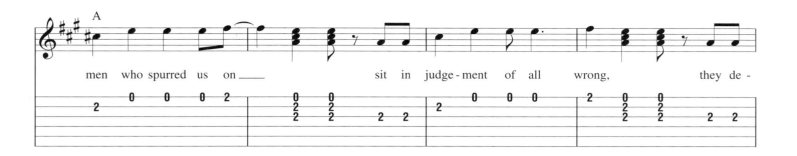

men who spurred us on ____ sit in judge-ment of all wrong, they de-

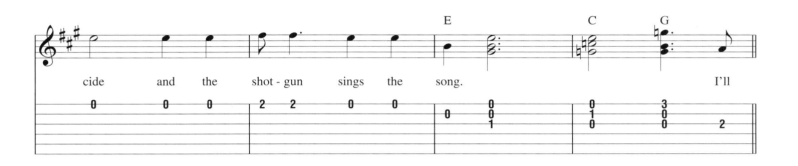

cide and the shot-gun sings the song. I'll

Chorus

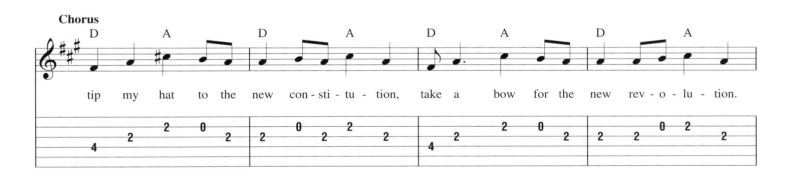

tip my hat to the new con-sti-tu-tion, take a bow for the new rev-o-lu-tion.

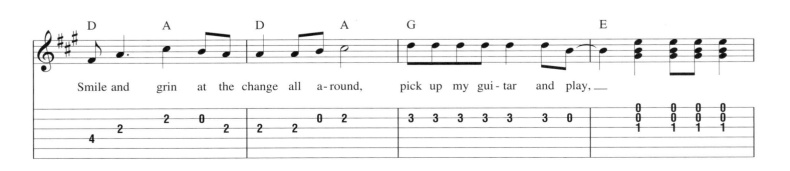

Smile and grin at the change all a-round, pick up my gui-tar and play, ____

just like yes - ter - day, ___ then I'll get on my knees and pray

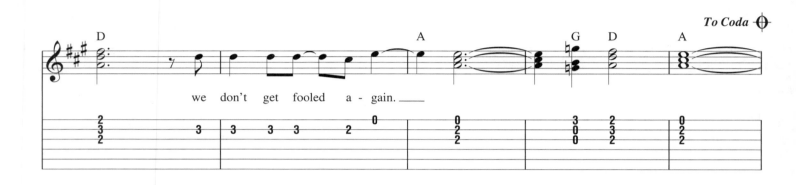

To Coda ⊕

we don't get fooled a - gain. ___

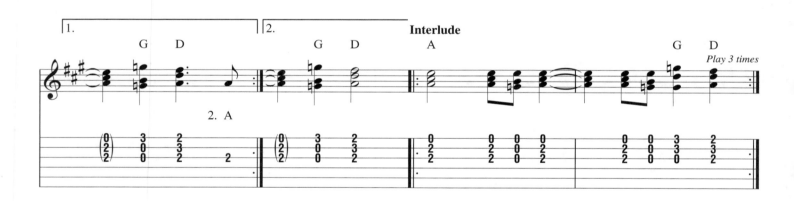

Interlude   *Play 3 times*

Bridge

I'll move my - self and my fam - 'ly a - side, ___

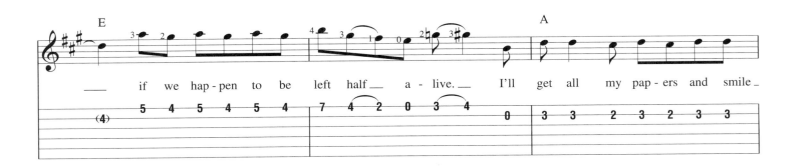

if we hap-pen to be left half __ a-live. __ I'll get all my pap-ers and smile __

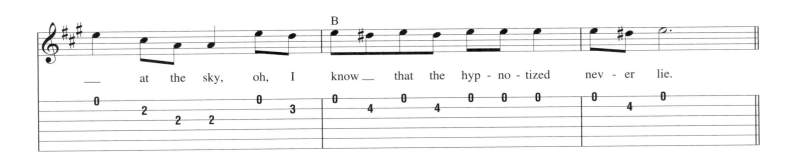

__ at the sky, oh, I know __ that the hyp-no-tized nev-er lie.

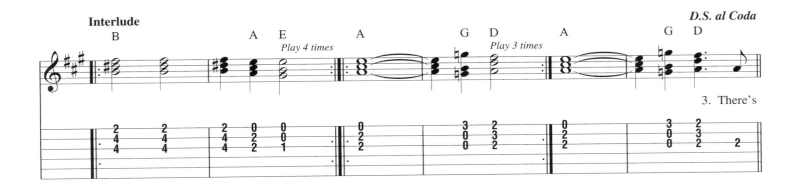

Interlude

D.S. al Coda

Play 4 times

Play 3 times

3. There's

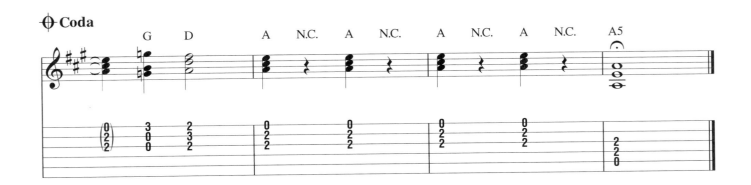

Coda

Additional Lyrics

2. A change, it had to come.
   We knew it all along.
   We were liberated from the fold, that's all.
   And the world looks just the same,
   And history ain't changed,
   'Cause the banners, they are flown in the last war.

3. There's nothing in the street
   Looks any different to me,
   And the slogans are replaced by the by.
   And the parting on the left
   Is now parting on the right,
   And the beards have all grown longer overnight.

Welcome Home

Words and Music by Claudio Sanchez, Michael Todd, Joshua Eppard and Travis Stever

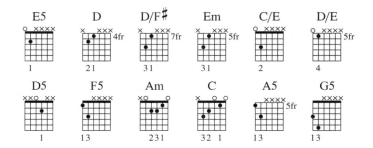

*Tune down 1/2 step:
(low to high) Eb-Ab-Db-Gb-Bb-Eb

Strum Pattern: 1
Pick Pattern: 4

Intro
Moderate Rock

*Optional: To match recording, tune down 1/2 step.
**Chord symbols reflect implied harmony.
***Seventh position

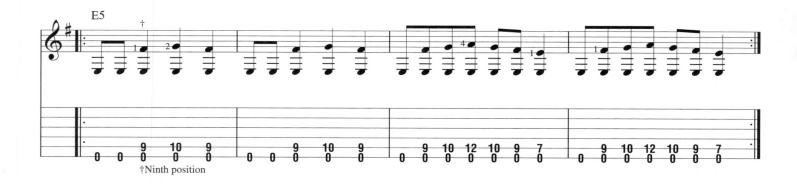

†Ninth position

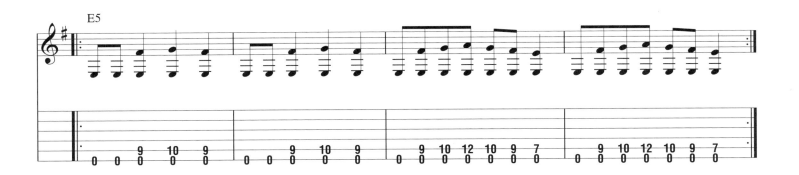

Verse

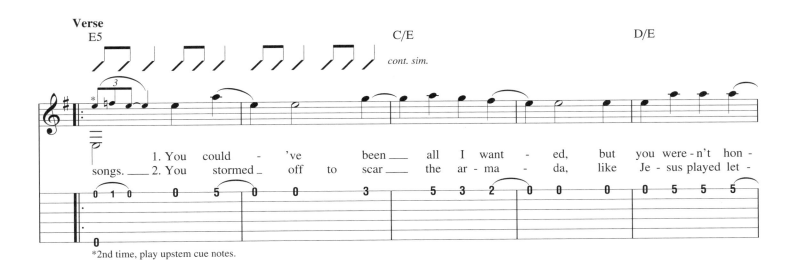

1. You could-'ve been all I want-ed, but you were-n't hon-
songs. 2. You stormed off to scar the ar-ma-da, like Je-sus played let-

*2nd time, play upstem cue notes.

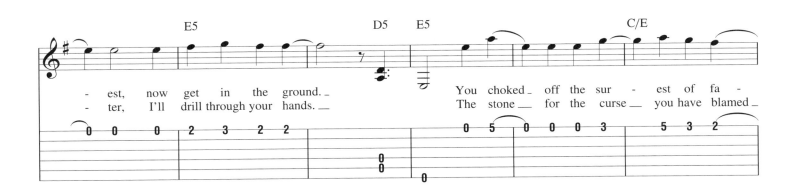

-est, now get in the ground. You choked off the sur-est of fa-
-ter, I'll drill through your hands. The stone for the curse you have blamed

-vors, but if you real-ly love me, you would've en-dured my world. Well, if you're
me. With love and de-vo-tion, I'll die as you sleep. But if you

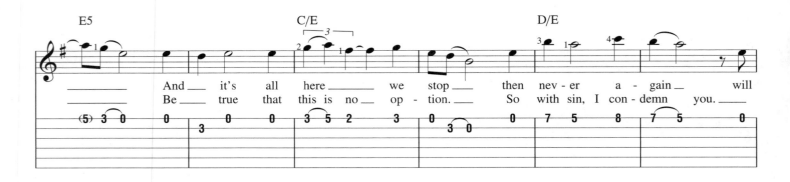

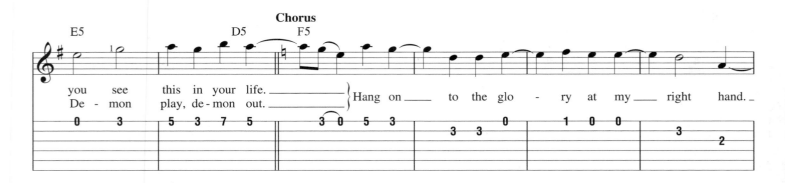

*One strum per chord, next 4 meas.

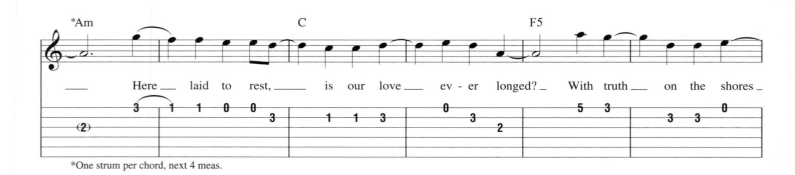

**One strum per chord, next 4 meas.

110

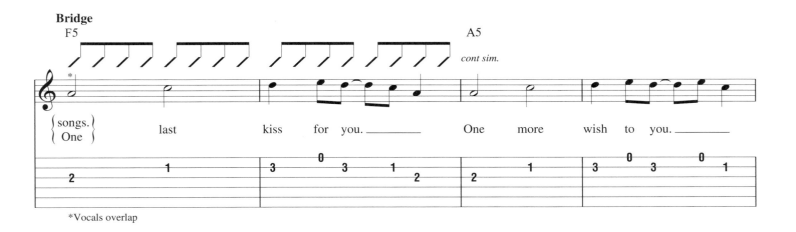

*Vocals overlap

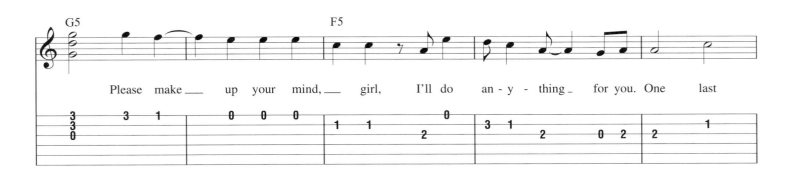

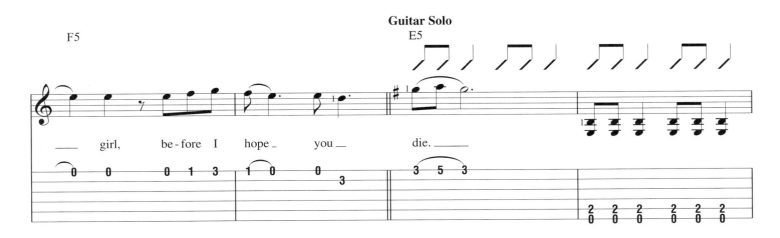